IT'S ALL ABOUT YOU!

It's All About YOU!

Finding Health, Happiness, and Love

Debra Stoltz

It's All about YOU!
Copyright © 2017 Debra Stoltz

For information, contact Debra Stoltz at soulbodynourishment@gmail.com

The content of this book is for general informational purposes only. The advice and strategies contained in the book are to be received with an open mind and may not resonate with everyone's opinions and beliefs. The instruction in this book is not intended to replace or interrupt the reader's relationship with a physician or other professional. Please consult your doctor for matters pertaining to your specific health and diet. Neither the author, publisher, The Institute of Integrative Nutrition (IIN) nor any of their employees or representatives guarantees the accuracy of information in this book or its usefulness to a particular reader, nor are they responsible for any damage or negative consequence that may result from any treatment, action taken, or inaction by any person reading or following the information in this book.

ISBN-13: 9780692863640
ISBN-10: 0692863648
Printed in the United States of America

Dedication

To my perfect partner:

Thank you for your patience, neutrality, kindness, generosity, support, forgiveness, and love. I express heartfelt gratitude for your sacrifice and commitment in helping me heal and start a new journey, coming from a place of service. You gave me the space and time to turn inward and change from being a victim to taking full responsibility of what was showing up and healing myself.

You have seen me at my darkest moments and now that I've climbed out of the darkness and am the light, you see me redeemed. Hallelujah! We have a choice to decide which path we walk down and which voice we listen to.

Thank you for respecting and trusting me in knowing that I can accomplish this now that I am awakening on my purpose-driven path.

Thank you for opening me up to all possibilities and what the world has to offer.

I look forward to sharing all the sensual pleasure of the earth on this journey together. I am eternally grateful for your showing up as my soul mate in tough times, giving me the opportunities to heal myself. Because of you, I have fought and won the internal war. I am authentic, awake, free, unlimited, all powerful, and the best version of myself now because of you!

My desire, as a healer, is to help others and give miracles to everyone I touch. It is my mission to share my love, tools, and tips to those who have a desire to understand what they feel and why their relationships have failed, how to succeed with the most important relationship of all, and how to find love, joy, peace, health, and happiness in the process. Thanks to my journey with you!

As always, I love you to infinity.

Acknowledgments

I wish to express my heartfelt gratitude to Monika Bury for inspiring me to write this book, partner with Myriam Dech to host a workshop, and inspire me to rename my business to SoulBody Nourishment. All of this has been possible because of her honesty and belief in me.

I wish to express my heartfelt gratitude to Lynn Feder, who has been an inspiration over the years and encouraged me to come out of hiding and facilitate A Course in Miracles (ACIM). We formed the Kingwood ACIM Study Group, and a beautiful group is now sharing its spiritual journey, love, and light.

I wish to express my heartfelt gratitude to Stephanie Tunks for putting up with my drama all these years, especially when I was "the victim" of my outer surroundings, and then for listening to all my newly learned information as I started on my journey of truth. Sometimes, I know she thought I was far out there, but I knew I was on the right path. Thank you for your true friendship, your patience, and being a good listener.

I wish to express my heartfelt gratitude to my mother, Anna Turner, who also put up with me and my drama while I was "the victim" in my relationship and crying out for help. As I started my journey, I would call her to ask questions about my childhood because I wanted to understand how to heal myself. She has always been there for me in her own way, whether I realized it or not. She has been patient and a good listener, allowing me to vent and release when I had nowhere else to turn.

I wish to express my heartfelt gratitude to my younger sister, Vicki Olsen, who is, much to my surprise, wiser than me in understanding truth and navigating through life. I appreciate her honesty and candidness when I would call her, desperately looking for help and playing the victim to what was happening in my life.

I wish to express my heartfelt gratitude to Lisa Manning for putting up with my drama during my massages, which I treated as therapy sessions, when I was "the victim" of my outer surroundings. It is because of her giving me a couple of books to read that the door opened toward the path of love. Thank you for caring enough to share the books, and thank you for believing in me. You are the thread to so many most beautiful, precious friends who are in my life now.

I am so grateful for the Lakewood Church Ministry and the Osteen family for all your service and a beautiful place of worship, online viewing, and ministry. Their sermons of positive thinking gave me hope when I was going through a time of depression in my life.

I would also like to thank the Institute of Integrative Nutrition for its support in helping build my foundation in wellness and health coaching and now for offering the Launch Your Dream Book course, in which I am creating this book. This course also has given me the privilege to meet my accountability partner, Linda McClead. I am so grateful for her friendship and continued support in helping me publish this edition. I know that the synchronicity of the universe brought us together and there are no accidents.

I would also like to thank everyone else who cared enough to give their time and love and helped with the realization of this book that will guide so many to finding love, health, and happiness.

Finally, I wish to express my total gratitude to my spirit guides, especially Jeremiah, who guided me in giving this book life.

CONTENTS

Introduction

My life was based on what others thought of me, and the "love" I received came from others externally. My family did not show much love in the way of hugs or saying, "I love you." I found love from others when they acknowledged something that I had accomplished. I believed that it was very selfish to put myself first, so I sacrificed my own needs and desires. As my way of feeling accepted and loved, I was always looking for ways to help others and then for their validation of a job well done. But when they were displeased or refused my help, their words and actions along with my own negative thoughts made me feel worthless and rejected. So I was always seeking ways to be acknowledged or helpful so I could feel worthy and loved. The grades, degrees, kids and their accomplishments, certifications, titles, volunteer positions, stature, and the like were defining who I was, and my purpose was seeking worthiness, love, and happiness externally.

I was a divorced single mom. I basically raised two kids on my own because their father passed away at thirty-five from a heart attack due to lifestyle. We lived in Kingwood, Texas, while our family lived in Fort Walton Beach, Florida, so I had only friends to depend on when I needed help with the kids. Both kids had their own "second families" that I could count on when I needed to travel for work. I was so grateful for the friends who helped us all the time. I also had been in a long-distance relationship for a long time, and I guess you can imagine the challenges that can exist with maintaining a long-distance relationship.

I finally became depleted and exhausted at forty-five, when my children were teenagers. I found an article called "Feel Better in Two

Weeks" that caught my interest because I was so desperate. Of course, being "superwoman" and constantly on the go, I decided I did not have the time to do what the article suggested and threw it aside. But I slipped and fell, twisting my ankle, which caused me to be propped up on the couch all weekend. I took another look at the article and started Googling, figuring out what the items were and which recipes I could cook.

After two weeks, and with the help of my daughter and her boyfriend, I was feeling better, so I kept doing it. This was the start to a new lifestyle of eating gluten- and dairy-free and only whole grains, which led to another book I am currently working on, *Nourishing Your Soul's Temple.* I thought food and exercise were the answers to all my problems but wanted to learn more about food, so I signed up with the Institute of Integrative Nutrition (IIN), where I received my health coach certification. This is where I learned about what we ate was truly secondary to primary foods. To be truly healthy, we need a balance in primary foods which consist of relationships, careers, spirituality, and physical activity. At this time, I realized I had no balance; I was failing at relationships, I hated my job and was eventually laid off, and I did not have a spiritual practice. I was only working out, loving Zumba and Pilates.

As the children got older, they no longer participated in the activities in which I had been involved, and they became more independent. I found myself with few friends, hobbies, or interests because I had devoted all my time to my kids' activities. I also had put my life on hold due to my long-distance relationship. I was desperately yearning for his love, happiness, and togetherness so we could start our life. I could not understand how he could love me and yet pull back, because I desperately wanted him to give me his love and make me happy.

I will admit that I had a hidden agenda of pushing marriage so I could stop punishing myself for having a relationship out of wedlock. I had a limiting belief that I was living in sin, and I was condemning myself for it. My health started to deteriorate, with stomach issues and constipation, and I eventually had a rectal prolapse and required surgery. At the time, I did not understand that my health issues were related to my beliefs about my relationship to my partner and money. In all honesty, I was looking for acceptance, worthiness, love, and happiness outside of myself and in all the wrong places because these were just temporary ways of helping me feel good.

My partner was the wiser of us because he knew that true love and happiness had to come from within by building a relationship with one-self. While he was waiting patiently, I was the victim of circumstance and fell into depression, lost my job, had serious health issues and sur-gery, and had to sell my home and personal effects. I was ignoring and avoiding this inner, deeper knowing, and I was suppressing my emotions because I was afraid and tired of hurting. I did not know at the time that I was making matters worse for myself.

My massage therapist recommended that I read *The Mastery of Love: A Practical Guide to the Art of Relationship* by Don Miguel Ruiz. This is a beautiful book, explaining love and relationships. I also remember when IIN said that fear did not exist. How could something that feels so real not even exist? I could not understand because it was real to me at the time. I am so thankful to both IIN and the book because they opened me up to asking more questions and taking responsibility for myself, which has led me on my spiritual journey to truth.

Since 2012, I have spent my time healing myself by learning how to build a relationship with my Higher Self by forgiving, loving, respecting, and honoring myself and letting go of limiting beliefs and past karmas. I no longer have to look to others for my acceptance, worthiness, love, and happiness. I also now have the most beautiful relationships with my friends, children, and partner because I love, honor, and respect myself. It is such a wonderful feeling to be free and to be filled with love, joy, and peace. I choose the path of love, and, yes, you can have heaven on earth! I now understand who I am in truth, what I am in truth, and how I serve in truth.

In this book, I will introduce you to yourself. No, not the one you think you know now, but the authentic one that God created that exists behind the mask that you have made. Right now, you have thoughts about who you are and what you are based on your ego's fear-based perception. You will gain an understanding of who and what you are in truth, how to change your limiting beliefs and thoughts about yourself, and how to learn to love yourself. You will understand how to heal yourself physically, emotionally, and spiritually by building a mind–body–spirit connection; eating nourishing, real foods; and exercising. As you learn to meditate, you will quiet down the monkey mind and build a relationship with your Higher Self. Just to clarify, we all have monkey minds that are the loud, endless chatters in the mind consisting of fear, anxiety, worry, and other negative emotions. You will start to understand that our physical manifestation is truly our separation from God, and it is all interconnected, with salvation being our only purpose. By building the perfect relationship with yourself, you will attract your perfect partner because like attracts like; being a universal law, this is so.

Because you have picked up this book and are reading it now, your soul is ready to hear the truth, whether you want to admit it or not. There are no accidents in this world. The universe is always working for the good of all, as you may have noticed in my aforementioned story— regardless of that loud voice speaking in your head right now that is saying negative things to you. Maybe it's telling you that you could never have these things or become this person, or that you do not have time to read this book now, or that this book is of no benefit to you. I ask that you read the book first before making such an abrupt decision. Right now, tell this loud voice in a loving way that this book interests you, that you want to read it, and that there is no harm in your reading it. You will have no regrets. It truly is an inward war, and this is the one war that is worth fighting. Make yourself a priority and love yourself enough to know that you are entitled to love, joy, peace, and happiness even when you do not know how or see the way. The secret is that your outer world is a direct reflection of your inner world.

I am sharing this information with you because I want your path to finding love, health, and happiness to be easier for you than it has been for me. Coming from a point of desperation and grasping at straws is exhausting, and you can feel defeated when there are not immediate results. If I can make a difference in someone's life because he or she read this book, then taking the time to write it has been worth it. You have a choice to invest in yourself, letting go of the past and any judgment, and to love yourself exactly the way you are right now. Only you can do this. As a wise friend once told me, if you do not take care of yourself, nobody else will!

As you learn to walk the path of love, you let go of all things that no longer serve you—judgment, guilt, shame, shyness, competition, hatred, fear, unworthiness, illness—and see a world that is filled with only love, joy, peace, and happiness. You become you by not worrying about what anyone else thinks because you come to understand that their perception is their own projection. You learn to take full responsibility of your own energy, thereby owning your power and truth. It really is all about you! As a Holy Son or Daughter of God, these things are your birthright for they are gifts from our precious Heavenly Father. So turn the page with excitement and anticipation of discovering the authentic you!

CHAPTER 1

GETTING TO KNOW YOURSELF

HAVE YOU EVER wondered who you are? Do you consider yourself to be male or female? A father or mother, husband or wife, brother or sister, or son or daughter? Maybe you think you are a doctor, nurse, accountant, manager, teacher, or lawyer. Or do you think you are a body, a soul that lives in a body, or even an energetic being of love and light?

Just ponder for a minute or two now and see what comes to mind. Turn to page 55 to write down your thoughts. There is nothing to be afraid or ashamed of, no matter what you think, so do not judge yourself or think that your thoughts are foolish. It's just that most of us probably have never slowed down enough to even wonder or ask the question. I will be honest in that I never thought about it for the longest time. Being honest with myself and others is something I did not do for most of my life because of who I thought I should be. As I continue to dig deeper to my authentic self, I am still questioning truth with myself at times. At various points in my life, I have been a daughter, wife, mother, nana, student, accountant, manager, Girl Scout leader, volunteer, certified health coach, and certified basic mat Pilates instructor, and I even passed all the exams to be a financial advisor, and I still felt inadequate and stupid. There was a void within that I just could not satisfy.

For those of us growing up in the United States, society teaches us at a very young age to be competitive and to judge ourselves based on our performance. We are programmed to join sports at an early age, and we go to preschool, grade school, high school, and on to college or a trade school if we want to amount to something. So we do what we are told and grow up with parents, teachers, and even coaches who compare us to our siblings, friends, and teammates. When we fail in their eyes, they teach us to also fail in our own eyes because these are the people we look up to and respect. We become filled with criticism, anger, humiliation, shame, guilt, shyness, negative thoughts, and even fear of doing "wrong." On the other hand, if we do well and are praised, then we think we are better than our siblings, friends, and teammates.

Each situation becomes an experience that molds you into who you think you are right now based on what you took away from the experiences. Watching TV shows, movies, and advertisements, or reading magazines programs you to think and determine your limiting beliefs because of the information you are receiving. Think back on your life and the memories you have, both good and bad. Think about how they impacted who you are today. Turn to page 55 to make a list of the best memories and how your life was impacted and turn to page 55 to make a list of the worst memories and how your life was impacted. It may or may not be obvious how they impacted your life yet, and that is OK because that is not the point at this time.

I hear your thoughts going through your head: *Oh boy, this book is going to be work and I do not have time for this, so I'm going to put it down.* But, before you do that, remember why you picked up the book in the first place. Something attracted you to this book. Maybe the title, *It's All about YOU!*, or maybe you are looking for something you have not found yet such as healthy relationships, love, filling a void within, feeling adequate, improved health, or happiness. Turn to page 56 to write down the reason you were interested in this book. All these years, you have been looking outside yourself for these things, depleting your energy, and you see where this has gotten you. You may have had failed relationships and failed jobs all because of how you think, feel, and look outside yourself for the answers. You have also looked to others for their opinions, acceptance, and love, thereby giving your power away to them. Heck, depending on your thoughts about money, you have probably also given away your power related to money. If you have any addictions, you have given your power away to what you are addicted to. These things control you by limiting your decisions about *when* you will do something or *if* you will do something. To find the things that you are looking for, you need to do some work. You are what you are and your life is what it is because of your current programming.

The best and most exciting news I can share is that the work is being done *to* you and *for* you so *you* reap all the benefits, and no one should put a value or limit on discovering love, health, peace, and happiness! I ask that you feel deep within and find the knowing that there has to be something better than where you are now. I know what it is like to be in your shoes. I also know how beautiful life feels once you do this work. Despite the fear or negative thoughts, find the courage to keep reading because *you* are worth it. Even if you do not believe it right now, know that I believe and trust that you truly are worth it! You are so important and matter more than you can ever imagine, so let's do this together by proceeding onward.

As adults, we even find ourselves measuring who we are in terms of worth by comparing ourselves to our coworkers or the family next door. We have been taught to think that because we have a bigger home, drive a better car, hold a certain job or title, or make a certain salary that we are better than the next person. We never feel content or satisfied and even feel envy or jealousy because others seem to have a better family, smarter children, or more material possessions. The point is, we are always judging ourselves and causing ourselves to never measure up to who we think we should be. We even create different images of ourselves that we master and use in different situations or around different people. This causes exhaustion, loss of hope and purpose, and loss of contentment and peace within ourselves. While you are on the path of fear, looking outside yourself and to others to complete you, you will never find true love, healing, or happiness.

In the United States, we are also measured by classes: lower, middle, and upper. So, unfortunately, people are judged accordingly. For example, to generalize, the middle class looks up to the upper class and feels envy and jealousy toward their material possessions, and we look down our noses at the lower class, judging them as "less than" and not socializing with them because of their looks, the cars they drive, or the jobs they hold. I just thought this was the way it was, so I was guilty as charged, allowing these emotions to fester within. If I encountered a lower-class person, I would avoid interaction and became filled with fear of being attacked or even robbed. Then I moved to Rotterdam and saw how people were treated equally no matter the job title. Everyone matters, and every position is necessary and respected. Even taxi drivers wear suits and drive Mercedes. Everyone takes pride in their work because they want to do a good job for their customers. This is something I think we have lost here in the United States if it did exist at some point.

Now look at your list of best and worst memories. Which one is longer? Some people have a "glass half empty" concept and remember the bad memories while others have a "glass half full" concept and remember the good memories. Again, there is no right or wrong. It just depends on your upbringing and the thoughts you focus on.

For those of us who have a glass half empty, which included me, we find the worst in most situations, we take criticism to heart, and we believe what these bad experiences tell us about ourselves. We feel we were treated wrongly, and our thoughts justify why this is so. We get close friends and family to sympathize with us as we justify being the victim. We allow these thoughts to fester in our minds, and they grow as we focus on them. These negative thoughts cause anger, hatred, and grudges that we hold on to. By hanging on to these emotions, we think we are blaming and punishing the person involved in the memory. But we actually imprison ourselves by believing these negative and now toxic thoughts that create limiting beliefs that hold us back in our ability to accomplish our dreams.

Can you relate? You may be high-fiving right about now, agreeing with everything that I've said here, justifying your behavior. I know that a few years ago that is what I would have done. But I want to let you know that this is a fear-based path that does not serve you; we will talk more about this later. Please know that these toxic thoughts are creating your current reality, including how you feel, your health, and limiting your ability to accomplish most things that you desire because you are not in alignment with Source, your Creator, and therefore not honoring your authentic self.

If you have a glass half full, from my observation, your focus seems to be on finding more of the positive in the experiences in your life. I am sure that you also have had some bad experiences that have affected your thoughts, limiting beliefs, health, and happiness. I am also sure that you have probably held on to some anger, hatred, or grudges that do not serve you because they limit your ability to accomplish your dreams. Again, I want to reiterate that this is a fear-based path that does not serve you, and we will talk more about this later.

Now, think back on a good memory on your list. I only suggest a good memory because it's easier to "own" our energy and take responsibility for the situation when it comes from good. We do not want to believe that we could create something terrible that has happened to ourselves. Do you remember how you felt before the event took place and leading up to it? Were you having happy thoughts and feeling good in general? Maybe you felt like you were on top of your game and this was a good time in your life, thus good things were happening. Would you agree?

I would like to point out, when thinking of either a good memory or a bad memory, that you have to agree that you felt a certain way leading up to the memory. The good memories occur when you feel good, which causes you to be in alignment with your authentic self, and the bad memories occur when you feel bad, causing you to be out of alignment with your authentic self. You are such a powerful creator that you are creating your reality based on your thoughts and emotions.

If you look around, you'll see that everyone has his or her own belief system, which creates his or her own reality. This is why two people can be involved in the same experience and yet have two different opinions. Sometimes you think to yourself when you hear the other person's version, *That is not how it happened. We were both there, and this is how it was*. This happens because of your different belief systems and because the cup-half-empty people are looking for the bad and the cup-half-full people are looking for the good in each situation.

The point is, our thoughts become programmed so that we walk around "asleep," forgetting the truth, and we use these programmed and fear-based thoughts in creating our outer world, believing and defining who we are and what we can accomplish. Obviously, there are varying degrees of how "asleep" each person is, based on his or her exposure to religion, media, past experiences, and the beliefs that were instilled in that person. Most of us believe we have no control over our life, so we walk around being an image that our ego has created and not recognizing our truth. That loud voice that you listen to now is your ego creating the fear-based thoughts, which you have chosen to listen to.

So, as a creative being that you truly are, you unconsciously create based on your programmed thoughts, whether negative or positive. My goal is to open you up to the possibility that you are more than just a body that has the power to control your thoughts, your emotions, and therefore your health and happiness. *You* are a soul, an energetic being of love and light made in the image of your Creator. You have a body, name, title, child, spouse, or credential. These are things you have. They are *not you*.

Most of us have looked externally to define and value ourselves, exhausting and defeating ourselves in the process. This search is never ending as well because what you are looking for does not exist outside yourself. As long as you follow the path of fear, believing the programmed thoughts and looking outside yourself for the answers, you will always be searching for love, health, happiness, peace, and joy because you are out of alignment with your authentic self. Your perception of the world around you is your state of mind that is reflected outward. This is why it is an internal war—the work is done *to* you, *by* you—and that's why it's all about *you*!

CHAPTER 2

A RELATIONSHIP WITH YOURSELF

WHAT KIND OF a relationship do you have with yourself? If you are not sure, what kind of thoughts or stories do you have about yourself? Just ponder for a minute or two now and see what comes to mind. More specifically, how do you treat yourself? Are you critical or loving? Do you punish or reward? Do you see yourself as beautiful or ugly, thin or fat, a success or failure, smart or stupid, worthy or worthless, happy or depressed, loved or unloved, abundant or deprived, privileged or denied, royalty or peasant? Turn to page 57 to write down in pencil on the broken line your thoughts about yourself. This is a time to be honest with what you really think. It is the only way to uncover the truth of how you feel about yourself. Avoiding the truth and suppressing your feelings is only extending your suffering and unhappiness.

If you want love, you have to practice love. Check in with your heart. Does it feel hard and cold or compassionate and warm? Turn to page 57 to write down how you currently feel. This is your measurement of where you are starting as you build a loving relationship with yourself. Again, no judging thoughts. This is just the ego telling you the thoughts or lies that you currently believe. If you want to have successful relationships with others, you have to practice building a successful one with yourself first.

We can learn a lot about being our authentic selves by watching little children under the age of four because their emotional minds and bodies are still healthy. They are still pure, so they live in the present moment and have not yet been programmed to be imprisoned by their past experiences, nor do they worry about the future. They are able to express themselves and are not afraid to show love. It brings a yearning to us when we watch them because they remind us of our truth. Unconsciously, we wish we could be like them, with no cares of the world. But I know that I remind myself that I am an adult who has responsibilities, so I discount these feelings, justifying how I think I should feel and behave. Feeling like I have to maintain a certain image, I let it go. Deep down, I feel saddened and let down. I suppress my true feelings based on how I think I should behave and act. What is the harm in expressing yourself and not being afraid to love? Maybe you are thinking that others may judge you or not accept your actions and behavior, so you will refrain from doing what feels awesome to you. *I choose to deprive myself just in case someone is watching and may say something rather than honoring me.* Well, sad to say, it's true this is what I thought and refrained from expressing my self.

I remember wearing only black or other dark colors just so I would not stand out, because I did not want to draw attention to myself. I remember not saying what was on my mind many times because I was afraid that someone would criticize or make fun of me. If I did say something, I always started with, "Well, I don't know, but maybe…" Because I did not want to be wrong or was worried about being laughed at, I discounted the value in what I was saying. Even saying "I love you" or giving hugs was hard for me because I did not grow up in an affectionate family.

I recently reacted to what a girlfriend said that surprised me. She says to another friend that "we have fun when we get together". I stopped dead in my tracks and said, "Who is having fun? Oh, not me." This is because I was programmed to believe that I could not have fun. It was always work before play, and play never came. You always had to work hard for the money, which was never much. So there was never any money or time for play.

After the work I have done on myself, my reaction surprised me. So building a relationship with yourself takes time. You are a work in progress. Check in with yourself now. What are some examples of situations in which you blocked yourself from expressing yourself and expressing love? Turn to page 57 to write down what prevents you from expressing yourself and love. Why did you react the way you did? Do you see how these thoughts are limiting your choices and creating your reality? As you become aware of your limiting beliefs and thoughts, you have the power to change your story. You are more powerful than you can ever imagine.

Do you blame yourself when things go wrong? Have you ever made a mistake? What sort of things do you say to yourself when things go wrong or you make mistakes? Turn to page 58 to write down how you talk to yourself when blaming yourself. Would you talk to someone else the same way you just talked to yourself? Probably not. I know that most people beat themselves up and put themselves down. They blame themselves for what happened when they think they have made mistakes. They allow anger to fester and do not forgive themselves or others easily. I want to share that, despite what we have been taught, mistakes do not exist. There are only opportunities to learn and to grow. All choices will lead to the same destination. Stop punishing yourself because this creates a disconnect with your Higher Self. It does not serve you. So please stop treating yourself and talking to yourself in this way. It is necessary if you want to find love, health, and happiness.

The following is a quote I love that was profound the first time I heard it during my health-coaching studies:

Our Deepest Fear[1]

Our deepest fear is not that we are inadequate. Our deepest fear is that we are powerful beyond measure. It is our light, not our darkness, that most frightens us. We ask ourselves, who am I to be brilliant, gorgeous, talented, fabulous?

Actually, who are you not to be?

You are a child of God. Your playing small does not serve the world. There is nothing enlightened about shrinking so that other people won't feel insecure around you. We are all meant to shine as children do. We were born to manifest the glory of God that is within us. It is not just in some of us; it is in everyone. And as we let our own light shine, we unconsciously give other people permission to do the same. As we are liberated from our own fear, our presence automatically liberates others.

To start building a relationship with yourself, go back to the list that you just made about what you think about yourself right now. Your current thoughts are probably ego based and are lies based on limiting beliefs from the programming we have been discussing. The *truth* is the opposite of everything negative that you wrote down. If you had positive thoughts in the list, then just relist the positive thought. For example, if you wrote "ugly" on your list, then write "beautiful" below it. Or if you already had "beautiful" on your list, then write "beautiful" down again.

Now, you may not believe this to be true because your ego will judge, but go through the exercise anyway and write down the positive words on the solid lines in red ink. You see, it is the truth because God created you in His image. This means you are made from love, so you are love. Your joy comes from extending love.

Read over your list now. Read the negative thought and then the positive thought. Do this repeatedly for a couple days. Now, erase the negative thoughts, and you are left with the truth. This becomes your affirmation sheet that is unique to you and your relationship with yourself. An affirmation starts with "I am _____," where the blank is your truth; for example, "I am beautiful." "I am" statements are powerful and, when stated daily, will shift your perception.

The next step is to state your affirmations daily using the "I am" statement before each truth about you. I recommend that you set your alarm about five to ten minutes earlier than your actual get-up time. When the alarm goes off, hit snooze and do a meditation with the thoughts in your mind. Run through the affirmations that are on your list. Use this time to set the tone of your day. Here are some examples: "I am energetic, excited, and healthy. All appointments flow with grace and ease." "I am stress-free, and time is on my side as I work on today's deadlines." "I love my life, family, and friends." "I feel safe in my relationship as I learn to trust and honor myself." "As I learn to appreciate myself more, I am seeing that others do too."

I accumulated these affirmations from listening to holistic healers. It's all about how you want to be treated and how you want your day to be. Remember your thoughts and emotions create your reality. Do this every day for at least twenty-one days to create a new behavior and to shift your perception. Keep doing it every day because it feels good to start your day on the right note.

After you wake up, go to the mirror and look at yourself. As the witness, just let any judgmental thoughts pass. Do not own them. In the beginning, there will be a lot. Say "I love you" and point at yourself in the mirror. Then hug yourself and say, "I love you" again. Do this every day and as often as you want. Allow yourself to receive and feel the love you are giving yourself so you can learn to love. Once you learn to love yourself, then you can extend this love to others. It is so wonderful once your love tank is full and you can share. In the interim, think of it this way, as stated by Matt Kahn. This is the best analogy for me, because, as a certified public accountant (CPA), I relate to numbers and money. Think of your love tank as a negative bank balance. As you add deposits, you do not feel much, but your debt is getting smaller. Eventually, you will break even and then reach a positive balance as long as you do not give up and you keep doing this every day. As you get to a positive balance, you will start to feel and recognize the shift. I do not suggest stopping even when you feel the shift. The more love you have to share, the more joyous you are.

Some other things I did to help me shift how I felt was to set a reminder in my phone that said, "I am enough and I love you!" During the day, I would see and read the statement. In times when I felt depressed or down, I looked at a picture of my dog because it reminded me of the unconditional love he always had for me, which shifted my mood and thoughts.

At the end of each day, complete a gratitude journal. Be grateful for what you noticed throughout the day and how you responded to situations, others, and yourself. Are you kinder, do you feel better, and does it seem that things are going smoother? Be the observer and witness. Become aware and own your energy, thoughts, and journey. Take full responsibility for yourself.

I also recommend reading *The Mastery of Love* by Don Miguel Ruiz. He explains what real love is and how to take responsibility for yourself. He explains that most people have codependent relationships because they look outside to others to meet their needs. You see, the key to any relationship is what you think of yourself and having the best relationship with your Higher Self. I read *The Mastery of Love* over a weekend, and I've read it at least three more times.

Remember, happiness never comes from outside of us. You are happy because of the love that comes out of you and you give to others. *The Mastery of Love* defines characteristics of love as follows, keeping in mind that the characteristics of fear would be the opposite[2]:

Love has no obligations
Love has no resistance
Love has no expectations
Love is based on respect
Love is ruthless; it doesn't feel sorry for anyone, but it does have compassion
Love is completely responsible
Love is always kind
Love is unconditional.

Not reacting to someone else's garbage is a test of your own self-love. Here is an affirmation that I got from Carol Tuttle, which you can also repeat daily as you learn to love yourself:

I recognize that when I feel upset, unappreciated, angry, frustrated, or resentful, there is a wounded part of me that is calling out for my love and support. It is my responsibility to heal and take care of that part of me, not my partners.

As I have been on my journey to loving myself, I have had many ups and downs and have even become lost as I learned how to truly love myself unconditionally. This is because I had given my power away at times by telling my partner that I wanted to go somewhere or do something. But when I tell him this, I expect him to take the initiative for us rather than owning my desire and taking the action myself. Remember that this is your desire, not the other person's, so if you want to start doing it or make the change, then you have to take the action.

Another way I became lost was by getting comfortable in our relationship and giving in to things because I wanted the relationship to work. The reality is that if you do this, then you are not doing anybody any favors. If you do not honor yourself in every situation, then you are causing yourself to be unhappy and disgruntled. Eventually, this becomes poison in your system. I recently was telling my girlfriend that I do not understand how I can be so happy around all my beautiful friends and yet be miserable in my relationship. I had my defining moment when reading *A Course in Miracles (ACIM)*.

Here is a recap just so you can understand where I am coming from.

I was laid off from work in 2013. My partner said that I could move to Rotterdam to be with him. Being together was the answer to my prayers, but it just was not on my terms. I struggled with it but eventually sold my home, my belongings, and moved to a foreign country, leaving my kids and family behind. For some reason I cannot explain, I felt defeated and powerless to him and money.

Anyway, I experienced a major health issue and had to have a major surgery. I knew that my relationship was a main contributing factor to my health issue, and I needed to address the root cause of the problem. So I moved back home to Kingwood, Texas. He was able to get a job transfer to Houston, Texas, but I told him that my focus was to heal myself and that I was my priority. How could I love someone else if I did not even love myself? We moved into an apartment. We got a dog, Sebastian, built a brand-new house, and created a beautiful home. Basically, I ended up losing sight of my priority: *me and my power.*

I got excited and comfortable in our relationship and did these things. I was even meditating and working on ACIM. But I forgot to honor my truth. I put on the mask and became the person who I thought I had to be to keep what I thought was a happy relationship. I found myself miserable and worse off than I had been two years prior. You see, I was honoring my authentic self around all my friends, and I was able to express my truth. I was following the correct teacher, Jesus, and listening to the correct guidance. I felt free, and my friends and I lifted each other up. But in the relationship, I was a different person, giving my power away and drinking alcohol for the wrong reasons. I was following ego and listening to that loud voice. I became miserable and disgruntled, and my health issues had not improved. My defining moment came from ACIM; it explained that as I tried to hold on to both teachers (Jesus and ego), it was causing me to go in different directions, creating confusion and causing me to lose my way. Always remember that *you* are the most important factor in any interaction and decision.

I owe it to myself and to everyone whom I come in contact with to be my authentic self, so I reclaim my power by being inspired by my book course accountability partner who provided me with some affirmations, which I have tweaked, to help me do so:

> I recognize and act on the best ways to take care of myself. Every day in every way I feel and look better; I am healthier and happier; and I love, honor, and respect myself.
>
> I am grateful that more and more I am living true to my God-given nature and I am loving it. I feel worthwhile and appreciated for being me.
>
> I am designing a life that I love.

I have sticky notes in my office with each of these affirmations to read every day as reminders. So how long does it take to build a relationship with yourself? I will not lie. It will take everyone a different amount of time to see improvement, depending on how much desire, determination, and intent each person has to change. All I can suggest is to not lose focus and to enjoy the journey because we are always evolving and expanding. Learn to love, honor, forgive, and respect yourself unconditionally. But never let your guard down and get comfortable in your circumstances. If you do get off course, give yourself a hug and tell yourself it is OK. Just look at where you are and where you want to be and make the changes to get there. At least now you have the awareness and tools to get back on track.

CHAPTER 3

CHOOSING A PATH OF LOVE OVER FEAR

How do you define love? Most of us are searching for love outside ourselves. We go on dates and get involved in relationships. We are so desperate for love that we try and make the person fit into our box of requirements. Initially, it's puppy love, so we love everything about the person and find no faults. Eventually, we fall in love, thinking we can make it work. It leads to marriage, having a family, and being together until death do us apart based on the marriage vows taken. Usually, these relationships are codependent relationships and not true love relationships. The powerful person in the relationship says, "I love you if you let me control you and if you will fit into the image I have made for you." The weak person, who is desperate for love, gives his or her power away and tries everything to please the other person. It's like having an addiction as mentioned in *The Mastery of Love* where the weak person has the addiction and the powerful person is the drug. You allow it to control you. This is selfishness, not love.

As time goes on, the weak person becomes unhappy and disgruntled because he or she cannot take any more abuse. The person still feels empty inside because he or she did not find true love. If you learn to love yourself and give self-love to yourself, then you do not allow selfish people to take advantage of you. This is why it is so important to understand the difference between the path of fear and the path of love. God has given you free will to choose which path you want to walk down.

We have relationships with everyone: our husband, wife, significant other, daughter, son, mother, father, brothers, sisters, friends, coworkers, bosses, and so on. As you interact with each person, you check in to see how the person reacts to your actions, words, and behavior. You allow the person's reactions to mold you into how you think you should act and even think.

> Every relationship we have is unique because we dream a small dream together. Just as your body is made by cells, your dreams are made by emotions. There are two main sources of those emotions: Fear and Love.[3]
>
> There are only two parts of your mind. One is ruled by the ego and is made up of illusions. The other is the home of the Holy Spirit where truth abides.[4]

The main sources of these emotions and the ones you relate to the most come from that part of the brain that you listen to. One is fear-generated emotions coming from ego and the other is love-generated emotions coming from love. While we experience both types of emotions, fear seems to dominate the majority of us. So why are most of us listening to ego, and why do we struggle with relationships and finding love? I think it goes back to our programming and past experiences that mold our beliefs about what we think love is. It's also being on the path of ego, where we look outside of ourselves for answers and compete against others. As we have these experiences and focus on these fear-based feelings, we accumulate emotional poisoning. Then we create rules to protect ourselves from emotional pain and from being hurt again.

Let's discuss the path of ego and these fear-based emotions now and check in with yourself to see if you resonate with this path. Go to page 59 to write down your feelings right now.

God, Our Creator, made us out of love, and so we are love. Our happiness comes from knowing when we are with God and extending our love. Grace is the natural state of every Child of God. As you have probably heard from the Bible stories, Adam and Eve ate the "forbidden fruit" of the tree of knowledge, causing a separation in the mind.

Eating of the fruit of the tree of knowledge is a symbolic expression for taking over the ability for self-creating.[5]

This is how the separation from God occurred. We now perceive ourselves as self-creating, but this is just a belief from the ego thought system from the ego mind. The Holy Spirit is the other side of the mind, which is our communicator to God, keeping us on the path of love.

The mind can make the belief in separation very real and very fearful, and this belief is the "devil." It is powerful, active, destructive and clearly in opposition to God, because it literally denies His Fatherhood. Look at your life and see what the devil has made. But realize that this making will surely dissolve in the light of truth, because its foundation is a lie.[6]

Thanks be to God! The only problem that ever existed was solved by sending His Son, Jesus Christ, who died on the cross and rose from the dead to save us of our sins.

It's time to understand which path you are currently walking down and which one you want to be walking down. Through free will, you choose which path to be on by which voice you choose to listen to and what you want your life to look and feel like. We go through life making our decisions and dealing with the consequences with either positive or negative outcomes. It's usually when we have had enough and feel at our lowest that we finally start questioning our life, our existence, and whether there is a better way. The quest and search begins, and our soul yearns for the truth.

I feel a lot of fear around making a decision, so I choose to procrastinate or avoid it altogether. Please know that if you do this as well, you are actually making a decision of not doing anything, which also has a consequence. I think the reason that I do this is because I am afraid of making the wrong decision. Please know that there truly are no wrong decisions. Each choice we make leads us on a journey down a path that is helping us move forward, learn, grow, and expand. Our human nature is to be content and comfortable. But our energetic nature is to always be growing and expanding. A beautiful quote I heard from my mentor while I was taking my health-coaching course at IIN is this:

Around every corner of fear is a miracle waiting to happen.

Think about it. Do you remember a time when you were afraid to do something? You tried to talk yourself into it—maybe jumping off a diving board or going on a roller coaster or swimming in the ocean—but once you finally found the courage to do it, you thought how much fun it was and how silly it had been for you to be filled with fear. You wondered why you waited so long to push through the fear. You actually punished yourself and let fear imprison you by preventing you from experiencing something new.

Now, maybe whatever you tried did not work out as you had hoped. That is OK, too, because now you have more experience and knowledge of what not to do, which you would have never learned had you not tried it. So, the next time fear creeps into your experience, remember to ask yourself what you are afraid of. Analyze the situation for safety, because sometimes the fear is a good thing and protects us. After you have objectively analyzed the situation, then go for it and find the miracle that is waiting for you.

Even after being on the correct path for awhile, it is easy to get distracted and get lost if you let your guard down. If you try to straddle both paths and have both Jesus and ego as your teachers, you will be confused and get lost. You have to unequivocally choose Jesus as your teacher so that you transcend ego. I explained in the last chapter that I was trying to straddle both paths and, based on the teacher I chose at the time, my experience showed up that way as well. So when I was with my girlfriends, being the authentic me with no judgment, my friends and I responded with hugs, love, and joy. We felt happy and free. But when I was with my partner and I wore my mask, being who I thought I needed to be for the sake of our relationship, both my partner and I felt pain and imprisoned.

As I continued doing this, the poison built up inside me, and the more frustrated and disgruntled I became. With this came hatred, judgment, and blame. I am so grateful for my defining moment when reading ACIM. Now I know that all I have to do is be the authentic me no matter what. Of course, that is always easier said than done. It is definitely a practice because we have been taught how to be on the path of ego, so we have to undo the ego teachings to find our authentic self of whom we were born. It is our nature to be love and to be on the path of love. That is why it feels so good to give and receive love. I think that is why love and smiles are also a universal language that everyone understands and yearns for.

Let us remember the definition of love in the Holy Bible:

Love is patient, love is kind. It does not envy, it does not boast, it is not proud. It does not dishonor others, it is not self-seeking, it is not easily angered, it keeps no record of wrongs. Love does not delight in evil but rejoices with the truth. It always protects, always trusts, always hopes, always perseveres.[7]

This definition is a good gauge to check in with. If something does not fit into this definition, then it is *not* love, so you need to choose differently to find something that fits into this definition as you work on healing physically, emotionally, and spiritually. Trust me, this definition will not lead you astray because it comes from God and it is what you are actually made of. It will feel right because it is your nature. Anything else is going against what you are.

CHAPTER 4

HEALING PHYSICALLY

So WHERE DO you start on your journey from brokenness to wholeness in an effort to be healthier, to be happier, and to find love? I started with healing physically—not because I knew it was a better choice than the other options but because it is what showed up to me first. I think this is because I have always been active and I liked being physical. The other reason is because my kids' dad passed away at thirty-five due to an unhealthy lifestyle. While he looked like he was in good shape, we did not eat our greens, so I figured I definitely needed to improve my diet.

I worked in an office, sitting at a desk every day. This is not good for the body. I always put the job and deadlines first. For fifteen years, I worked for the same company, sacrificing my personal well-being and family relationships for the job. My dad had been in the military, so I thought I had to go above and beyond, not understanding boundaries and balance. The only physical activity I had was chasing after my kids and doing things with them.

My son joined karate after his dad passed. I thought this would help him learn respect and anger management and give him a role model. He excelled at the sport, and we were spending so much time at the studio that I thought I would join the classes rather than sit on the sidelines, doing nothing. I always wanted to learn karate from the time we lived in Okinawa, but my parents said it was a boys' sport and enrolled me in ballet instead. I did not like ballet, and I quit. Anyway, I made it to an intermediate level in karate but struggled doing flying side kicks and got bruises on my hands from breaking the boards, so I quit again...

After getting laid off after fifteen years, I joined a gym and started going to a 5:30 a.m. Pilates class. It worked out great with my schedule because my son was in middle school at the time, but it only lasted for a few months until summer, and then the class was cancelled. I loved Pilates. I remember my coworkers telling me that I had the worst posture and that I would be the little old hunched-over woman. It was that bad. But, over time, my core became stronger. My posture and balance improved. As I felt stronger in my body, I also felt more confident and happier with a more sculpted body. I stood taller with my chin higher, actually making eye contact with others.

I had believed that no one liked me, so I did not have many friends. What I did not realize is that my posture, with my gaze to the ground and my feelings about myself, put negative vibes out to others. As soon as I felt better about myself, making eye contact and smiling at others, I started talking to people and making friends. Proof is in the pudding that our past experiences and what we believe are what show up around us. You listed the lies that you think about yourself in the exercise from chapter 2, and you might want to look back at them to see if you have anything more to add when thinking in this perspective.

With me, there was still a problem that I could not quite put my finger on. It felt as if I were making a wall between me and the friends I was making, and my shoulders were still rounded forward even though my posture had improved. My Pilates and yoga instructor finally told me that my rounded shoulders were due to a wounded heart and that I was protecting it. You see, I had a traumatic past experience in my relationship with my partner in which, at one point, I felt as if I'd been stabbed in the back and right through the heart with a dagger. It caused muscle spasms down my back for a week. I had wanted so desperately for him to propose and for us to get married. He led me to believe this was going to happen during one of his visits. I had my hopes up so high that I was completely devastated, with a crushed heart, when he left without proposing. Wow—I could not believe that my emotional wounds were showing up in my body language and affecting me physically.

I got another job and found a great workout schedule that allowed me to go to Pilates and Zumba back to back three times a week, but I was not eating healthy or allowing time for self-care. I eventually felt depleted and exhausted, with no more gas. I found an article that read "Feel Better in Two Weeks," which was the start of my lifestyle change to eating greens and whole grains and eliminating wheat, dairy, chemicals, preservatives, additives, and the like from my diet. It took time to figure out what ingredients like quinoa, millet, buckwheat, and lentils were as well as what recipes to cook, but I did.

Over several weeks, I started feeling better. I wanted to keep doing it, so I kept figuring out new recipes. My friends noticed my increased energy and weight loss (which was just a by-product of wanting to feel better) in Zumba and asked what I was doing. This led me to creating my next book *Nourishing Your Soul's Temple*. If I was going to help others with changing how they eat, then I wanted to know more about food and why my menus and recipes worked. This led me to IIN where I received my health-coaching certification. I loved how I felt with these changes to my diet and exercise so much that I believed that it was all that was necessary to find health and happiness at the time. I even got my certification as a basic mat Pilates instructor so that I could help others reap benefits such as building their powerhouse or core strength to support the spine (which is your lifeline), improved posture, improved balance, more energy, more confidence, increased lung capacity, and more.

We are made of energy, and energy has to move or it becomes stagnant. Exercise, in any form, moves energy, thereby creating more energy in the body. Even just focusing on your breath moves energy in the body. It is not about the quantity of what you do but rather the quality of how you do it and the intention that you set for the workout. It is also about the thoughts that you own during the workout. As one of my yoga instructors, Lynn Feder, once said about a balancing pose, "If you think you cannot do it, you are probably right. But if you think you can do it, you are also probably right." This is so true. When I first started working out, I remember thinking *This is so hard. I can't do this.* Then I started changing the dialogue in my head during my workouts to *Thank you for showing up and moving; this feels so good. Thank you; you can do this. You are doing awesome, and you are getting better and better.* Sometimes, I would even do affirmations: *I love you. I am awesome. I am strong. Every day in every way, I am getting better, better, and better.*

In yoga class, the instructor mentioned that our spine consists of seven major chakras, which is the anatomy of our spirit. There is a root chakra, sacral chakra, solar plexus chakra, heart chakra, throat chakra, third eye chakra, and crown chakra. My interpretation of the location of each is as follows:

1. The root chakra is at the base of the spine.
2. The sacral chakra is right below the belly button, the abdomen.
3. The solar plexus chakra is above the belly button, stomach, and solar plexus area.
4. The heart chakra is heart and lung area.
5. The throat chakra is the throat and cervical plexus area.
6. The third eye chakra is at the brows area with gaze to the tip of your nose.
7. The crown chakra is the top of the scalp area.

Chakras are subtle energy centers that correspond to the seven major nerve plexuses in our physical body. Each energy center governs different aspects of our physical body, our spirit, our personality, and our life. The more we meditate, the more we can emit the qualities of the different centers.[8]

It is not my intent to go into great detail here about the chakras; you can Google and find so much information on the Internet. The point I want to make is that we are energy and we have chakras and meridian points throughout the body that make up our energy body.

Each chakra correlates to different organs in the body. When these chakras become impacted by experiences, thoughts, and beliefs, then aches, pains, and eventually illnesses show up in the body. Disease is actually *dis-ease* in the body because your body is trying to get your attention to make a change. I was dealing with a lot of digestive issues that were related to the solar plexus chakra and were associated with my relationship issues. I had major surgery, which helped my immediate physical health issue, but I knew now that in order to heal myself, I had to resolve the underlying issue surrounding my relationship.

I did not understand that discomfort in the body was the body's way of getting my attention. I was taught that it was hereditary or that I was getting older so it was appropriate to have joint pain, arthritis, digestive issues, thyroid issues; to become overweight; and so on. I remember growing up and being told that I took after the Turner family, my dad's side of the family. I thought this meant I would be overweight and at one point I was gaining weight. But when I released the belief and started loving myself, I changed my story to being healthy and fit. These are all limiting beliefs, and if you want to change something, you have to first change your belief about it. Are you listening to your inner guidance system? What are some limiting beliefs that you would like to change? Go to page 60 to write them down.

You also need to honor yourself and listen to your body because the body is a communication device that the Holy Spirit uses to guide you. The Holy Spirit cannot force anything upon you due to free will, but you do have a choice to pay attention and listen. Anytime you feel any discomfort, it is the Holy Spirit's way of trying to get your attention. The change you need to make is not always obvious, but you need to check in and be honest with yourself.

Do you eat to live? When you think about it, it is a profound thought. I think most people today do not eat to live. They eat what tastes good and what is available fast. They do not think about the ingredients and the nutritional value. God made our bodies and He made natural food to nourish our bodies. Do you think about what type of gasoline you put in your car? Probably, because you want to make sure your car is going to work and take you wherever you want to go. Well, it is the same for your body. It is your vehicle for your spirit to take you on your soul's journey to awakening. Food is energy, and it nourishes your body to the extent of the nutrients in the food you consume. It's like the saying "you are what you eat."

Soy and corn are genetically modified organisms (GMOs) and wheat has been hybridized over the last fifty years, thus increasing its gluten content exponentially in the United States. Processed foods like white rice, white flour, and white sugar are stripped of their nutrients. Foods are also doused with pesticides, chemicals, and preservatives. Our health is adversely affected by all these concerns and modifications because the food is no longer natural, whole foods. This is why there are so many health issues today.

Three of the top ten causes of death which are Heart disease, Cancer, and Diabetes[9] are all related to gluten sensitivity.[10]

Understanding what you are eating and checking out the labels is imperative for your health. If you cannot pronounce it and if you do not recognize the ingredients listed on the label, then I do not recommend buying it. It's back to the basics in my kitchen cooking with organic, whole foods whenever possible.

We are all interconnected with everything because God made everything. The body knows what whole food is and knows how to process the nutrients to provide healthy cells and energy to the body. We just need to become aware of the causes of our health issues and to realize that going back to the basics of eating food from nature can make a big difference in our overall health.

I never could appreciate or understand why people prayed over their food until recently. Not only am I grateful for the abundance that surrounds me, I also pray that the energy that has gone into the food from producing, providing, and even preparing it is made whole so it nourishes my temple with only positive effects. The production of meat consists of the environment the animal is brought up in, the food it eats, the conditions it lives in, if it was given antibiotics, and so on. It is so sad to see how factory farming treats the animals. My recommendation is to eat humanely raised animals and only wild caught fish in moderation.

The production of grains, vegetables, and fruits is impacted by genetically modified organisms, chemicals and preservatives to make it last longer, and additives to make it look and taste better. Corporations have chosen profit over the health of individuals. I did not understand this until I moved to Rotterdam. There was a fast-food place that served the same milkshake in Europe as in the United States. While Europe required the company to use real fruit in the milkshake, and they did so to comply, the same company in the United States chose to use flavorings because they were allowed to do so.

Also, food in Rotterdam is fresher, spoils faster, smaller in size, and tastes better. All the additives and preservatives that are allowed in the United States are not allowed in Europe. I was even able to eat at a French bakery because the gluten was not supersized in the laboratory. I have heard other friends state that they can go on vacation in Europe, eat bread, and lose weight. The only way we can change our food in America is to quit buying from the corporations and go back to supporting organic farm-to-table options. Organic food is the natural, normal food my grandparents and parents grew up on. Everyone says that they cannot afford to eat organic, yet they can afford to go to the doctor and pay for prescriptions. I say that food is my medicine, and I choose to heal from the inside out. I am investing in my physical health now so that I can be healthy as I age and enjoy my whole life to the fullest.

I hear so many people tell me that they do not have the time to work out or go back to the basics of cooking. Actually, I was one of those people telling myself the same thing. Remember, you always find the time and the money to do what you decide is important to you, and your thoughts create your reality. If you want to feel and look good, you have to honor and take care of yourself. Only you can do this. Yes, it can seem overwhelming. Rather than focusing on the whole picture, decide on one small step you can make today toward exercise and eating healthy. For exercise, maybe you can take a walk in nature, or you can take the stairs instead of an elevator, or you can park farther away from the store to take more footsteps. For a change in diet, maybe you can replace a candy bar with a carrot or a soda with a glass of water, or you can add a green vegetable to your plate. Depending on the changes you are making, you might be able to make a new change each day or each week. Set up a plan that works for you and stick with it.

I remember one time when I wanted to jog a mile, I was so out of shape that I could only jog for a minute or two before I had to stop. But I was determined to prove that I could do this, so each time I jogged, I pushed myself to go just a little bit farther. Eventually, over a period of time, I was able to run the mile. Another time, when I had not jogged for a long time, my partner wanted to jog around the track at the gym. By the way, we both had big egos. So we started jogging around the track. Neither of us would be the first one to stop, so we kept pushing each other until we ran a mile. I could not believe that we did it nor do I recommend it. In a situation like this, the ego did not have my best interest at heart, and I could have gotten hurt since I was not used to jogging.

Once I was exercising and eating healthy, I thought that this is all there was to being healthy. Yet, I was miserable in my job, depressed, and feeling lonely. While I was in IIN, I discovered that our health is also attributable to our primary foods of career, relationships, spirituality, and physical fitness and what we ate was truly secondary to our overall health and well-being. I had only one of the four primary foods working for me. I believe my depression came as a result of my limiting belief surrounding my relationship with my partner. This impacted my motivation, energy, drive, enthusiasm, relationships with kids and friends, and productivity in my job. I was a complete victim, being helpless. At the time, I did not understand how to own my power and take responsibility for me and my half of the relationship. I prayed every day for us to be together and for the truth in my relationship with my partner. The universe answers in unexpected ways and, of course, not the way I wanted. So my journey continued forward to show me that our physical health is interconnected with our emotional and spiritual health, which is discussed in the next chapters.

CHAPTER 5

HEALING EMOTIONALLY

HOW DO YOU heal emotionally? I never knew that I needed to heal or even could heal emotionally until recently. We have an emotional body just like we have a physical body. Just because you cannot see it does not mean it is not there. The physical body, emotional body, and spiritual body were intended to work together to support each other when God created them. However, this is not the case anymore, and they are working independently of each other. This makes it more difficult for our emotional healing process. God did not create us to suffer, and yet so many of us are in constant suffering, with so much emotional pain. We have been trained to suffer by learning to follow the path of ego by society, parents, teachers, and the like. This suffering comes from the ego and believing that we are the body.

Most of us hold on to grievances because we have been wronged, and we push down and ignore our feelings because we do not want to feel the pain. This does not serve us and is affecting our physical health. It just weighs us down like we are carrying the weight of the world on our shoulders. The more we carry, the lower our energetic vibration is. It is necessary to forgive and let go of grievances in order to stop punishing yourself and release yourself from the past so that you can be free to live in the present. It's also time to allow the suppressed feelings to surface so that you can release them once and for all.

The planets in the universe are actually helping us let go of all the karma that we have been holding on to. That is why we feel so much turmoil when the planets are in retrograde. God and the universe know that we are too weighed down, and they are helping us release so we can become lighter. Most of us just do not understand what is happening, and we feel like these are challenging times to say the least. Yet we have many great opportunities to allow suppressed emotions to surface so that we can release them and allow lessons to present themselves so we can forgive and learn the lessons at hand. The universe is preparing us for ascension but we have to let go of everything that no longer serves us to raise our energetic vibration before we can ascend.

An important tool to help heal emotionally is journaling. Our ego is good at making up untrue stories. Journaling helps us dig deep down past the superficial thoughts to how we really feel. Once you understand how you really feel and why you feel this way, then you can start making changes to heal emotionally. One of the tools I learned from IIN is called Morning Pages. You sit down in the morning and just start writing everything that comes to mind with no judgment for about an hour. Then, you go back and read what you wrote. You will be amazed by what eventually shows up if you allow the flow of writing whatever thoughts come up.

Another tool that I use is a gratitude journal. At the end of each day, before bedtime, I write down at least three things that I am grateful for. These can be small things, like a smile or feeling the sun, or more significant things, such as something being done for you or the opportunity for you to help someone else. You hear a lot about gratitude journals and that it is important to be grateful. This helps us recognize the abundance that already surrounds us and can help shift a lack mentality.

I found that the gratitude journal helped, but I still was not appreciating and loving myself unconditionally. I was still feeling like I had not done or given enough. I was always critical of myself and judging myself. Finally, I decided to start an appreciation journal. At the end of each day, I write down all the things I did that I could have appreciation for. I recognize generosity, self-care, taking care of my dog, helping someone, spiritual nourishment, physical nourishment, hugs, smiles, and so on. This helps me realize how much I am already doing for myself and others that I am not giving myself credit for. It helps me shift how I feel about myself as well as accept and love myself.

Emotional freedom technique (EFT) is an energetic way of healing emotionally. It's a type of tapping on the meridians, which are energetic points in our bodies. They are smaller and there are a lot more of them than the main chakras mentioned in the last chapter. While tapping on certain points, you express statements based on what you are trying to heal. It is effective, and I have used it to heal from past relationships and past childhood trauma. You can learn more at www.thetappingsolution. com, where Jessica and Nick Ortner offer a lot of information and free resources.

Healing emotionally includes paying attention to who you are spending time with and how they make you feel. Do they build you up or tear you down? I have such a beautiful group of friends now who always build me up and support and encourage me but it has not always been this way. I thought I was healed and moving forward because I see the love and friends that surround me. I thought I was strong enough to face anything for any length of time because I understood that lessons present themselves for the opportunity to learn from them. I am stronger and more determined, but I think that there comes a point when being around others that constantly cause you to react becomes poison to your thoughts and emotions. You know it is poison when you let it bother you and when you feel you cannot shake it. You start to lose your enthusiasm, feel defeated, and nullify your feelings. This is not a healthy way to be around people, a significant other, or in certain situations that cause you to feel this way if you are not strong enough to address how you feel.

You have your own perception based on your thoughts and beliefs about any relationship and yourself. This is what shows up in the dream that you share. When you are neutral to what shows up, then you know that it is their garbage and not yours. But when you react, then you know that you have your own inner work to do. When this happens from time to time and you are in the right frame of mind, it can be a great opportunity to learn a lesson. But, when it is coming at you constantly to the point you cannot breathe, think, feel good, or be you, then you owe it to yourself to choose the company you keep carefully—remember, it is a choice and it is up to you. Know that you are important enough and matter enough to care 100 percent about how you feel at all times.

To not honor and respect your feelings causes harm to your emotional and physical bodies. Deep down, you know better than to allow another person to affect your mood and emotions, yet you do it anyway. Maybe you think you deserve to be treated or talked to this way. You blame yourself, which makes you feel bad, so now you feel bad and think bad things. You become hateful, spiteful, or vengeful, fighting back to stand up and protect yourself. The funny thing is, this makes you actually feel worse, not better. Have you ever stopped and noticed? You see, you have chosen the path of ego during this interaction. As you think you are being hurtful to another, you are actually harming yourself.

As you ignore your true emotions—which, remember, is your inner guidance system—you become more disconnected and disgruntled with your Higher Self. Then you eat foods, drink alcohol, or take drugs to suppress your emotions and to get through the days and weeks. Eventually, you feel groggy, in physical pain, lethargic, inflamed, depressed, angry, and disappointed. The good thing is that you recognize the situation you are in. Awareness is one of the first steps in being able to make a change. You know that your thoughts control your reality and that your emotions control your vibration based on the universal law of attraction which says:

That which is like unto itself, is drawn.[11]

Focusing on negative (lower vibrational) thoughts brings about a more negative experience, while focusing on positive (higher vibrational) thoughts creates a more positive experience. It is so easy to slip back into habits and run on autopilot, especially when you have been a victim for so long and you know the role so well. Another key factor is to observe how you feel when you are around others. I came to realize that I felt awesome around almost everyone. This was a clue for me that I needed to address my relationship with a few people because it was not serving me. Here are two quotes from Charlie Chaplin[12]:

> As I began to love myself, I found that anguish and emotional suffering are only warning signs that I was living against my own truth. Today, I know this is Authenticity.
>
> As I began to love myself, I freed myself of anything that is no good for my health—food, people, things, situations, and everything that drew me down and away from myself. At first I called this attitude a healthy egoism. Today, I know it is Love of Oneself.

Most of us were not taught to listen to our emotions and to love oneself, but this is what we need to do to come into alignment with our truth and heal emotionally and physically. If you want to be happy and feel good, it has to start with letting go and forgiving yourself and others for everything that you are holding onto. As you learn to forgive and let go of the past, then you learn to pay attention to how you feel and honor yourself as these feelings present themselves so that you can stay emotionally and physically healthy.

I know now that my journey has been challenging because of the limitations I had placed upon myself. I came to a personal revelation about my journey while journaling, and I will share this with you now to give you hope, inspiration, and strength, because I know that your journey is also an uphill battle and the place where you are probably feels impossible.

I choose love.
I am love.
I extend love.

As I extend love, love comes back to me. As I am open to give and receive love, I realize it has always been there, all around me. I was just blocking it because of my unforgiven past experiences, thoughts, and limiting beliefs about myself and the world around me.

The more I forgive, allow, recognize, and appreciate love and all the abundance that already surrounds me, the more abundance shows up in my life.

The more I follow my intuition, instead of that loud voice in my head, the better I feel about myself. Through forgiveness I am able to free myself from the hell I have created. I now reach out and share thoughts, help others, give kindness, and extend love.

CHAPTER 6

HEALING SPIRITUALLY

ARE YOU SPIRITUAL? I never thought I was. But even though I was not dedicated to a church or religion, I believed in angels and I listened to Christian music. Although I could not understand it or see it, I knew that there was a force larger than me. I remember when my kids asked the dreaded question, "Is Santa real?" my response was, "If you believe, then you will receive," and we just left it at that. I always felt a magic around Christmas, in this holiday built around believing, giving, and the birth of Christ, Our Savior. It is my favorite time of year.

Regardless of your religion or beliefs, you can be spiritual—that is, believe in spirit and a larger force beyond your physical self. Once you start asking the questions "who am I?" and "why am I here?" your soul is seeking spiritual truth and expansion. Your soul needs nourishment just like your other bodies. Spiritual nourishment comes in many forms. There were times when I was nourishing my soul and connected to my flow without realizing it. These were times when I would volunteer, donate, help others, work in the yard, go to Zumba classes, read the Bible, go to church, and listen to Christian music because it made me feel good. In Houston, KSBJ 89.3 FM is the radio station for contemporary Christian music, which has been my lifeline through a divorce, the passing of my kids' father, two layoffs, and all the other curveballs life has thrown at me. Now, with an understanding of truth, I have added yoga, meditation, focused breathing, and facilitating ACIM to my list of my spiritual nourishment.

Growing up, I did not have a religion. I was embarrassed to say I was "nothing" when someone would ask what religion I was. So I made sure my kids and I went to church, and they were baptized when they were young. Still, I was filled with pain and depression and was desperately seeking help outside of myself. I went to a chiropractor, acupuncturist, massage therapist, and another chiropractor, and I took many vitamins and supplements. At one point, I had a whole shelf filled with natural herbal remedies.

My massage therapist knew my pain and was wiser. Over time, I built up a relationship with her and trusted her. She suggested that I read *The Anatomy of the Spirit* and then *The Mastery of Love*. She then invited me to her home for an ACIM study group. The books introduced the truth about who I am and how to turn inward and heal myself. Because I was so desperate, I was open to anything that could possibly help me. While the material was eye-opening and hard to accept, because I believed I was a body, I remained open because nothing I had done up to this point was working. She had this peacefulness about her that I wanted for myself.

I also quieted down the loud ego thoughts and learned to check in with my heart. How did I feel when I read the book? How did I feel when I forgave myself or someone else? How did I feel when I made a twenty-one-day commitment to changing a habit or a thought that was not serving me? You see, you cannot describe in words your connection to the divine and your truth. You can get out of your own way and allow the Holy Spirit to use your body, which is its communication device, to guide you on the path of love.

Once my kids became young adults, I started asking myself questions like the ones in the last paragraph because I felt so empty and unfulfilled inside even though I had a great job and a great home and was building up all my earthly treasures. But, while I was asking these questions, I also felt fearful of what might show up and also of allowing feelings to emerge. I avoided being alone and I suppressed my feelings. My soul, however, was yearning to get my attention because I have an important mission and purpose during my lifetime, as we *all* do. Yes, every one of us is very important, needed, and necessary in God's plan for our salvation. It took my selling my home and all my belongings, tucking my tail between my legs, and giving my power over to money and my partner and moving to a foreign country for my soul to get my attention. I felt defeated, fearful, lonely, and hopeless. I had been praying for five years for God to bring my partner and I back together because my love and happiness came from our relationship. I also prayed for the truth because I was unsure about our relationship; if I was going to have the relationship, I wanted the truth. Well, have you heard the phrase "be careful what you wish for"? You may have a specific idea of what you are asking for, but it may mean something different to the universe, and you might not get what you expected. I wanted the truth about our relationship, and I got the truth about life and about me:

Who I am in truth
What I am in truth
How I serve in truth

When I was laid off, I could no longer afford my home, and my partner said that I could move to where he was living. I was in shock and arguing with God that these were not my terms. I had meant that my partner come to where I was. I finally accepted the move as being God's plan, and I tried to trust as I let go of everything. I was in shock. My partner kept saying to be ruthless by releasing attachment to my physical earthly treasures that can be replaced. Letting go was the hardest thing I have ever done because of the materialistic attachment I had and the value I placed on my belongings. Yet it was the best thing I could have done for myself at the same time because I learned to understand that we do not build our treasures on earth but rather in heaven. Also, by letting go of the old, I allowed space for the new.

I always said that when I turned fifty, my life would change. I wanted to have my kids by thirty so that by the time I was fifty, they would be independent so that I could do the things I wanted to do. I just had no idea that I would start my spiritual journey and start seeking out my purpose. I think I now understand midlife crises in which people feel empty inside and they buy extravagant items to find satisfaction in their search for fulfillment outside their self.

When things are going well, most of us think we are managing great and do not need any help. It seems that it is only in times of difficulty that we stop and take the time to pray, asking for help. This is how we exercise our free will, and when we choose to be in control, God cannot override our choices. It is through the prayer of relinquishment that we are able to surrender our control over to God and allow Him to take control of our lives. Two quotes from an article called "The Prayer of Relinquishment" helped me say the prayer and release my free will.[13]

> ...I came to the same point of abject acceptance. **I'm tired of asking,** was the burden of my prayer. **I'm beaten. God, you decide what you want for me...**
>
> ...brings Jesus' prayer into focus for us. **Dear Father, all things are possible to you. Please let me not have to drink this cup. Yet it is not what I want, but what you want...**

For a lot of us, this does not happen until we are worn out and exhausted from our failed attempts of trying to do it on our own. Things become a mess; maybe we experience depression, suffer financial loss, go through a divorce, lose our home or job, experience health problems, and so on. It is when we finally fall on our knees, realizing that there has to be a better way, that we relinquish our control in a prayer to God. He is gladly waiting to help, but you have to let go of control first.

After I moved, I was in an environment where I knew only my partner, and he worked and traveled a lot. My only connection to anyone else was through the Internet. Somehow, I started discovering tools to help me learn how to meditate and find truth, but it was like I was trying to brainwash myself, and I wanted quick results. I was so desperate that I was buying tools and trying them in hopes that they would work. I spent a lot of money and built up a nice toolbox that I now use to help others no matter where they are on their soul's journey.

So, I would get impatient and frustrated, which was a form of resistance in itself. I was not connected to my heart. It felt so hard and cold. The only form of unconditional love I could feel that kept me going was by looking at a picture on my phone of my dog, Sugar Ray. He was actually a dog my daughter had adopted. When I was laid off, he came to hang out with me because I was home during the day so I considered him my dog. He went back to my daughter when I moved to Rotterdam and he came back to me when I returned home. Sugar Ray passed away in October 2015 from kidney failure, but he will always have a special place in my heart. I read on Facebook once that "dog" spelled backward is "God," and that dogs are gifts from God to teach us unconditional love, forgiveness, happiness, and how to enjoy the moment.

Sugar Ray in 2013 before I went to Rotterdam.

I remember crying out to God and pleading with Him quite often because I could not understand why I was in a place where I felt all alone. Why was this happening to me? I was so desperate, wanting love, joy, peace, happiness, power, respect, honor, and worthiness. At one of my lowest points, I took a picture of a sunrise from our window of our condo on the thirty-first floor. I noticed later the cross in the picture made out of the clouds. This beautiful message from God reminded me that He does exist and I am *not* alone, ever. It gave me hope and faith to know that He was with me, that He was in control, and that everything was going to be OK. I actually felt a sense of peace and love fill my body.

Beautiful sunrise overlooking port of Rotterdam
with a message from God: a cross.

Now that God had my attention, I started trusting the process more. I used all the tools that showed up and listened to all the interviews that came through my inbox with the intent of loving myself, forgiving myself and others, letting go of past karmas and traumas, and enjoying the journey.

As you take your spiritual path, you will begin to question everything you have learned in order to understand truth. If it comes from God, it is truth, and if it comes from ego, it is part of the illusion, which is a lie and therefore does not exist. Here is a quote from *A Course in Miracles*[14]:

Nothing real can be threatened.
Nothing unreal exists.
Herein lies the peace of God.

So, you see, if God did not create it, then it cannot be real. Since God did not create ego, and it is formed by separation in the mind, it is not real. The ego makes up all the negative thoughts and lies so they are not real either. This takes you back to your chapter 2 exercise in which you explored what kind of relationship you have with yourself. Know this:

When you lay the ego aside, it will be gone. The Holy Spirit's Voice is as loud as your willingness to listen. It cannot be louder without violating your freedom of choice, which the Holy Spirit seeks to restore, never to undermine.[15]

It's time for you to take responsibility for your life and know that what you are currently doing is not working for you. Your soul's desire is the truth and is urging you to listen and act according to the guidance the Holy Spirit provides.

The journey to God is merely the reawakening of the knowledge of where you are always, and what you are forever. It is a journey without distance to a goal that has never changed. Truth can only be experienced. It cannot be described and it cannot be explained. Jesus can make you aware of the conditions of truth, but the experience is of God.[16]

Now, you just have to find the courage to take the first step, trust that the universe is supporting you, and have the faith that your soul's best interest is at heart.

I created meditation prayers that have been very impactful to both myself and my study group that I would like to share with you. The first meditation prayer is connecting with Jesus as your teacher and companion. This meditation references the seven major chakras that run up the spine that were described back in chapter 4.

The second meditation prayer is understanding that you are not a physical body; rather, you are a soul that lives in a body.

Please go to page 61 for the meditations. Please note that the meditations include material from ACIM chapters that apply to our Kingwood ACIM study group.

CHAPTER 7

ATTRACTING YOUR PERFECT PARTNER

DO YOU DREAM about your perfect partner? Have you gotten involved in a serious relationship only to find out that he or she is *not* your dream partner? Do you go on countless dates and feel like there is not a perfect match out there for you? I think a lot of people are searching for the perfect partner and keep coming up disappointed. Maybe even out of the desperation of not wanting to be lonely or thinking they cannot find anything better, they settle and find themselves miserable. I know that I thought I would never find anyone else who would love me, so I married my first husband. Two beautiful children came from the marriage, but unfortunately it ended in divorce because we got married for the wrong reasons and did not understand who we were and what unconditional true love was.

I think too many people are lonely and desperate, so they jump too quickly into sexual relationships without building a relationship first. Again, they are searching outside of themselves for love, happiness, and fulfillment. Granted, it takes time to go through the process that I am suggesting, but the investment is worthwhile to get the most out of your next relationship. I believe that you should get to know yourself first, and then each other, while making sure you are being your authentic self and not settling for anything less. If you pretend to like things that your partner does, and you do not honor your authentic self, you will always find unhappiness and disappointment. You focus on "If I don't like this, he or she will break up with me." Well, would you rather sacrifice and be unhappy, disgruntled, and unhealthy or would you rather honor yourself and find true love and happiness? The choice is yours to make. Don't let fear of the unknown or judgment of failure or feeling inadequate hold you back. Remember, these are the ego's lies. Maybe you need to revisit the exercise in chapter 2 and add more lies to the list, following with the truths and affirmations. Once you realize that your joy and happiness comes from loving yourself so much, you will not accept anything less than what honors your authentic self. As long as you try to be something you are not and try to push a square peg into a round hole, you will never find what you are looking for.

While you are working on becoming your authentic self, I recommend reading *The Mastery of Love* by Don Miguel Ruiz. It explains what real love is and how to take responsibility for yourself. You see, the key to any relationship is what you think of yourself and having the best relationship with your Higher Self. Remember, happiness never comes from outside of us. You are happy because of the love that comes out of you. Love has no obligations, no resistance, no expectations. It is based on respect. It does not feel sorry. It is completely responsible. It is kind and unconditional. In order to find a healthy and happy relationship, you have to understand who you are, how to honor yourself, and what true love is.

Now your thoughts are becoming more positive because you have created your affirmation list and are repeating them daily. You now understand what true love is, and you are learning to love, appreciate, honor, and respect yourself. You are feeling better and lighter because you are healing emotionally and you are feeling better because you are exercising the body and providing nourishment for your soul and its temple. You are discovering how to be your authentic self with no worries or judgment as you shift your thoughts to truth. You may notice that more people are talking to you and noticing a change about you. Your vibration is increasing, and you attract people according to your vibration. The more you love, appreciate, honor, and respect yourself, the more love you extend out to others. This is a natural state of being that cannot be helped.

It is time now to make a list of your dream partner's qualities and traits by turning to page 65 for the exercise. You need to go deep to your soul level, pushing aside ego and the self-made images of what you think this person should look like and any thoughts of what someone else thinks you should like or do. Don't discount the first thoughts that enter your mind because usually those gentle thoughts are truth, with ego telling you that they are not possible. You may be asking what this has to do with finding the perfect partner. Well, the truth is that what you become is what you attract. By making the list from the heart, you know that this is coming from your authentic self and what you are willing to accept and not accept. You have to trust that the universe is going to deliver the perfect person as you become the person you want to attract. Tune in to your heart.

Go to page 66 to do a creative visualization meditation in which you visualize yourself being with your dream partner. The brain does not know the difference between actually doing something and visualizing doing it. See yourself doing the things you both love to do. It's like the saying "ask, believe, and receive." Most of us ask but do not really believe that it will happen, or we lose hope because it did not manifest fast enough. What you believe is the foundation and key to what shows up in your life. This process will take some time, but it will bring you the perfect partner because of law of attraction: like attracts like. Establish your desire first, and your actions will follow. You will see the powerful and great creator that you really are!

Look at your list. How many of these values or traits do you already have, and where are you lacking in the list? The latter are the areas you need to work on. Most of us look outside ourselves for all the answers, and we are hoping that someone else can complete us by bringing to the relationship what we think we do not have. You have to look within yourself for everything and find your truth. As you discover your truth and become your authentic self, all your desires and needs are met. Your perfect partner and you are like a key that fits into a keyhole perfectly.

The next suggestion is to add some affirmations to your affirmation list that will help you not only in the relationship with yourself but also with your perfect partner. Here are some examples that came from Carol Tuttle:

> I am learning to build a relationship with myself, love and respect myself, honor my own needs, know my worth and power. I am learning to follow my intuition and get on the path of least resistance.
>
> As I continue to learn to appreciate myself, I am seeing that others do too. I recognize the ways that others show love to me.
>
> I give genuine compliments effortlessly and accept compliments with thanks. I am moving forward with my life in a way that supports and honors me.
>
> I am experiencing more and more support. I am enough. I count. I am creating a relationship of mutual support, understanding, and joy. I am loved deeply and authentically.
>
> I recognize that when I feel upset, unappreciated, angry, frustrated, or resentful, there is a wounded part of me that is calling out for my love and support. It is my responsibility to heal and take care of that part of me, not my partner's.

The purpose of the affirmations is to shift your focus and thoughts about yourself. As you change your focus and thoughts, you change your beliefs. Your thoughts are energy, so positive thoughts put out a higher vibration than negative ones. But you also have to look at how you feel when you have these thoughts. Your thoughts and emotion join to create a feeling that is a stronger vibration than just the thought or the emotion on its own. As you love yourself and take better care of yourself, you will feel better about yourself and thereby raise your energetic vibration. It comes back to the law of attraction that I already mentioned.

Now, what if you feel that you have attracted the wrong partner(s) and are feeling frustrated? Take a step back, find a neutral space, and turn to page 68 for the next exercise. You may not like what you see in this exercise. It is only with honesty that you are able to truly find what you are looking for. I had a friend who is desperate for her perfect partner tell me that a person is not able to get all the qualities that he or she wants in a partner, so she has been settling with each boyfriend. In settling, she finds only temporary happiness and eventually realizes that she is unhappy and that it is not going to work out long-term. These are limiting beliefs.

As you become the best version of you, your perfect partner will appear. If you do not want to wait that long, then you need to understand that everything that happens with your chosen partner is all about you, and you have to take 100 percent responsibility for turning inward and healing your wounded child. If you are not ready to do this, then I suggest that you keep working on you.

You have come a long way just since picking up this book and working on the exercises. Remember that it is a practice to untrain the brain of the lies and retrain the brain with the truth. Look at how many years it has taken to get to where you are. It will likewise take time to change. You have already taken the hardest step by admitting that there has to be something better and finding the courage to seek it. Remember to focus on just one step at a time and to love yourself no matter what happens. There are no mistakes, just opportunities to learn, to grow, and to expand to our truth. There will be more opportunities to learn, grow, and expand until you finally learn the lesson. It's definitely a process, but you are worth it. You are of utmost importance over anything else! If you keep a gratitude journal or an appreciation journal and look back over it, it will remind you of the progress you are making. Sometimes this is helpful when you feel down. It is a good reminder that you are on the right path.

CHAPTER 8

THRIVING IN A MATERIALISTIC WORLD

WHAT DOES YOUR world look like? The one I lived in was very materialistic, meaning that I measured love by my success, because this is when I received attention, and I measured my worth by the titles I had and the things I owned. I also made my decisions based on fear that held me back from things I wanted to do. I thought the solution to my desperation of feeling love and happiness came from my relationship with my partner. The more I grasped at him to give it to me, the more he pulled away, leaving me feeling rejected and unloved.

I think my children received more love in the home growing up than I did as a child, because I told them I loved them, whereas my parents did not tell me they loved me. Because the kids' dad passed away when they were five and nine years old, they received a Social Security payment to help support them. I made sure it was used on them so I believe they were taught to be materialistic. They experienced doing activities, traveling, and buying things they desired. Today, I am trying to explain to them that materialistic things are not what is important in life and that love and happiness have to come from within.

Did you think about what your world looks like? Are your days chaotic and over scheduled? Do you feel drained, overworked, and out of control? Do you feel alone with the weight of the world on your shoulders? Do you recognize which path you are walking down? Are your choices giving you life or taking it away? *You* decide what your day looks like and *you* have the power to create a balanced and beautiful day by what you choose your commitments to be. Allow this to sink in because it is truth.

Sit down and look at your schedule for the week. Where can you insert a meditation at the beginning or end of the day? Where can you fit in some self-care treatments? How about setting reminders in your phone to Ask the Holy Spirit for guidance or to remind yourself that *you* love yourself and that *you* are enough just the way you are? Also, as we said in an earlier chapter, you set the tone for the day as you are waking up with your affirmations before getting out of bed.

Do not be afraid to say no when someone asks you to do something if you do not have the time or feel that you cannot offer 100 percent of yourself to the commitment. You are doing both of you a favor by saying no. You are listening to ego if you feel guilty and act against your better judgment. Whatever decisions you make, accept and honor the decision that you have made.

Yes, there is still a materialistic world around us, but we have a choice to exist in this world without being of this world. Because our society still uses money in exchange for goods and services, we will continue to use money for our needs and desires for the time being. But note that the energies are shifting, and the financial structure, which is currently vibrating at such a low vibration, cannot and will not sustain itself. It is too low of a vibration and too many people have given all their power over to it. It is one of the idols that the Bible warns us about and this low vibration does not serve us as we ascend to a higher consciousness.

Thou shalt have no other gods before me.[17]

What is your relationship with money? When you give your power over to money, drugs, cigarettes, alcohol, and so forth you have put another god before our Father, God. The financial structure along with our educational structure and probably the government will eventually collapse because all their vibrations are too low for ascension. People believe that money is their livelihood. Success is measured by money and money separates us in America into classes. I was taught that you had to work hard for money, that I was not worthy to have a lot of it, and that it did not grow on trees. These are all just limiting beliefs. Money is just a piece of paper with a number printed on it. The only value that it has is what you give it.

It is my goal to come from a place of service as I take 100 percent responsibility for myself and as I ascend in consciousness. As we become our authentic selves and know that we are whole, perfect, and complete, we do not worry about what is in it for us because we have transcended the ego. According to our truth, we just want to come from a place of service and give with no expectations of getting anything in return. We just have the joy in giving to or doing for another. What freedom it is to know that you do not have to feel guilty if someone does something nice for you and there is no obligation that you have to do something in return unless you want to.

It is time to detach yourself from money or anything else to which you have given your power. Free yourself from it by letting go now and reclaiming your power. The attachment to these things is weighing you down and holding you back from your ascension. The lessons surrounding your attachment to these things will continue to present themselves until you can release your attachment to them. Releasing your attachment is an ongoing process and a lesson I have been working on for a while. I see improvement and know the process is working. As I let go and reclaim my power from money, I feel more empowered and free. As a reminder from the Holy Bible:

> Do not store up for yourselves treasures on earth, where moths and vermin destroy, and where thieves break in and steal. But store up for yourselves treasures in heaven, where moths and vermin do not destroy, and where thieves do not break in and steal. For where your treasure is, there your heart will be also.[18]

Are you building up your treasures here on earth or are you building your treasures in heaven? I know now that by building my treasures in heaven, they are there for eternity. The love, happiness, joy, peace, abundance, energy, gratitude, appreciation, and support I feel is so much more valuable than my earthly treasures. The void and emptiness within me that I felt for so long and my attempts to look outside of myself are disappearing as I honor my truth and allow my authentic self to be expressed. My love cup is overflowing now and I share this love and light with everyone that I touch because I see people for who they really are. I no longer see the self-made images of the body that we have created and believe that we are. Another reminder from the Holy Bible:

> Jesus said unto him, Thou shalt love the Lord thy God with all thy heart, and with all thy soul, and with all thy mind…Thou shalt love thy neighbour as thyself.[19]

This is more powerful than you may realize because we are all *one*. We are all the One Son of God in the Sonship. It is only through separation that we think we are separate. The way we treat a brother or neighbor is what you believe about yourself. The next time you have a bad thought or treat someone badly, check in with why you thought, felt, or acted this way. I remember being in Rotterdam and feeling so full of hatred. I went on to say how much I hated my partner, and then I quickly turned it around and said that I really hated myself for letting my career go and for allowing myself to become powerless to money and to him. It was a wake-up call about how I was not listening and honoring my true feelings and then lashing outwardly, inflicting pain on him and then back on myself.

The more you love yourself, the less you worry about what other people think about you because you are not looking outside yourself anymore for love or acceptance. As you discover your authentic self, you accept yourself just the way you are, knowing that you are exactly the way God made you: whole, complete, and perfect. You discover freedom by giving yourself permission to be *you*. I remember wanting others to like me so much that I wore many masks just trying to fit in. In one of Joel Osteen's sermons, he says that if these people do not like you, then you are looking in the wrong place. Don't take it personally, and keep moving until you find the right people who accept you for who you are.

There are people here in this world who are here to help you and those who you are here to help. If it does not feel right, then it is not. Do not try to force things to fit in. This is ego and the frustration comes from not listening to your authentic self, who is trying to guide you along the path of least resistance. We just have to listen. This helped me change my perspective in understanding my feelings, honoring myself, and looking for my authentic self. Eventually, as I loved myself and found things that I loved to do, I found the most beautiful friends in Zumba, Pilates, and yoga.

The more you love and honor yourself, forgive yourself and others, and let go of all things that no longer serve you, you will become your authentic self. You will feel free, confident, elated, joyous, excited, energetic, powerful, and limitless. It is the most awesome feeling to no longer feel imprisoned by doing things that truly do not serve you. As you are living your God-given nature, you are the observer and witness to what is going on around you. You choose to listen to the Holy Spirit rather than following and listening to ego, which causes you to react to everything around you.

Please Google and listen to a beautiful heartfelt song I love called "Come Holy Spirit" by Bryan Duncan. Then give the function of judgment to the Holy Spirit so that you will see the false ideas of the ego for what they are and lay them aside. As you interact throughout the day, ask the Holy Spirit for true perception of anything that is questionable or that does not feel right. Please see page 69 for a Holy Spirit prayer meditation. Always come from a place of neutrality so that you do not set yourself up for disappointment. Also, neutrality enables you to get out of your own way so that the Holy Spirit can use the body as a communication device, which is its intended purpose.

You have a teacher, companion, and communicator guiding you now on the path of love. Remember to check in and listen to your inner guidance system often when making decisions for only The Holy Spirit knows what is best for you. Leaning on your own understanding and making your own decisions by listening to the loud voice only causes you harm as you have already witnessed with your past.

When making decisions, does your body feel restrictive? This is my no response. Does the decision feel expansive in the body? This is my yes response. You can tune into your body as well. Ask yourself a question that you know is a big no and see how you feel it in your body. Now do the same for a big yes and see how you feel as well. Now you have a sense of your body's communication guidance to you when asking questions you do not know the answer to. Remember, it does take time to really get a sense of listening and feeling your inner guidance. Be neutral, have faith, and trust the process as you practice and learn to connect with yourself.

Remember to acknowledge your evolvement, growth, and expansion while on your soul's journey so you are measuring your progress. This is your proof that what I am telling you is truth when ego tries to tell you otherwise and words cannot really describe it. You have to feel your way to trusting your Higher Self and building the most important relationship you will ever have.

Exercises and Meditations

Chapter 1

Make a list of who you think you are.

_____

_____

_____

_____

_____

_____

Make a list of your best memories and how they impacted your life.

Memory	Impact
_____	_____
_____	_____
_____	_____
_____	_____
_____	_____
_____	_____

Make a list of your worst memories and how they impacted your life.

Memory	Impact
_____	_____
_____	_____
_____	_____
_____	_____
_____	_____
_____	_____

What attracted you to this book? Be honest with yourself.

_____

_____

_____

_____

_____

_____

Chapter 2

What kind of relationship do you have with yourself now?
This concept came from Lisa Nichols but I am not sure what she called it.
Write what you currently think in pencil on the broken lines. These are the *lies*.
Write the *truth* in red ink on the solid lines.

_____

_____

_____

_____

_____

_____

Measure your starting point by filling in the blank.
My heart feels _____.

Write down some examples of when you have blocked yourself from expressing yourself and expressing love? Why did you react the way you did?

_____
_____
_____
_____
_____
_____

What mistakes have you made or what things went wrong and what did you say to yourself?

Mistake	What You Said to Yourself
_____	_____
_____	_____
_____	_____
_____	_____
_____	_____
_____	_____
_____	_____

Chapter 3

Make a list of your feelings right now.

_____

_____

_____

_____

_____

_____

_____

Chapter 4

List the limiting beliefs that you want to change.

_____

_____

_____

_____

_____

Chapter 6

Meditation Prayer Connecting with Jesus

Sitting tall in a comfortable position, take in a deep breath, completely filling your stomach, lungs, and chest. Pause and let it out completely exhaling pressing the belly button to the spine. Again, take a deep breath in and let it out, pulling the belly button to the spine.

Now close your eyes as you inhale and exhale. Breathe in and out, focusing on the breath and the tip of your nose. Follow the breath going in and out as you settle down, breathing in and out. Connect to the breath as you breathe rhythmically and become more relaxed. You are now relaxed.

Focus on a beautiful golden light coming down from the heavens and into your crown chakra. Focusing on your crown chakra, say quietly in your mind as you envision an infinity symbol (sideways eight), "I am in you and you are in me." As the light moves to your third eye, say, "I am in you and you are in me." As the light moves to the throat, say, "I am in you and you are in me." As the light moves to the heart, say, "I am in you and you are in me." As it moves to the solar plexus, say, "I am in you and you are in me." Moving to the sacral chakra, say, "I am in you and you are in me." As the light moves finally down to the root chakra, say, "I am in you and you are in me."

Now visualize your heart chakra opening up and Source light coming out and filling the room, providing you with safety and protection. Call upon Jesus and ask him into your heart. Wait quietly with expectancy for Jesus's presence.

Let Jesus know that you accept Him as the Atonement (cancelling out of all errors that you could not otherwise correct). You are forgiven and the inner light within you shines away darkness. Being filled with spirit, you forgive in return.

You choose to unite with Him as your teacher and companion, knowing that when you unite with Jesus, loneliness is gone and you unite without the ego. You also want to unite to His mind and with His will.

Now ask for His strength, making you invincible. Say, "I can do all things through Christ who gives me strength."

Ask for His guidance and help, knowing you are alike. As you join with Jesus, know that God's power is restored because you are uniting with God.

Feel the love of God shine upon you with this beautiful light that surrounds you and accept God's glory, joy, and peace now because of your acceptance of Jesus.

Reach out and grab Jesus's hand, letting Him lead the way and transcend the ego.

Give gratitude for Jesus our savior, the atonement, and salvation.

Pause now and sit quietly for a minute.

Slowly come back and become aware of your surroundings. Turn your palms down and move your hands and feet. Open your eyes when you are ready.

Mediation Prayer for Understanding That You Are Not a Body

Sitting tall in a comfortable position, take in a deep breath, completely filling your stomach, lungs, and chest and let it out completely exhaling pressing the belly button to the spine. Again, take a deep breath in and let it out, pulling the belly button to the spine.

Now close your eyes as you inhale and exhale. Breathe in and out, focusing on the breath and the tip of your nose. Follow the breath going in and out as you settle down, breathing in and out. Connect to the breath as you breathe rhythmically and become more relaxed. You are now relaxed.

Bring to mind a tranquil place that makes you feel relaxed. Maybe you envision a beach, a garden, a waterfall, or something similar. Feel your surroundings: the air, sand, water, or grass. Hear the noises: birds, waves, or water falling. See your surroundings. Are there flowers, trees, sand, and water?

Allow a beautiful white light come down from heaven and enter your crown chakra and move down into your heart. Move your focus from the mind down to your heart center. Open your heart and allow this light energy to expand and surround you. Feel the warmth and support of this energy. Know you are safe and completely relaxed in the light.

Call upon Jesus, who is your teacher and companion. Wait quietly with expectancy for Jesus's presence.

As you speak to Jesus, say,

"Please help me remember that sickness is a way of demonstrating that I can be hurt and that it is a witness to my frailty, vulnerability, and extreme need to depend on external guidance."

"When the ego attempts to bring me to sickness, please help me remember NOT to ask the Holy Spirit to heal the body, because this would merely be to accept the ego's belief that the body is the proper aim for healing. Remind me, rather, that I ask the Holy Spirit to teach me the right perception of the body because perception alone can be distorted."

"Please help me understand that I am equating myself with a body when any form of attack enters my mind, which is the ego's interpretation of the body. If I use my body for attack, it is harmful to me. If I use my body only to reach the minds of my brothers who believe they are bodies, then the Holy Spirit can teach His message through me, reminding them that this is not so. I will also understand the power of the mind in me."

"Please help me remember that the Holy Spirit uses the body as a communication device to end separation and communicate our unity in the one mind we all share. This heals my brother and therefore me."

"I am one Self, united and secure in light, joy, and peace."

"I am God's Son with one Creator and one goal: to bring awareness of this oneness to all minds that true creation may extend allness and the unity of God."

"I am one Self, complete, healed, and whole, with the power to lift the veil of darkness from the world, and let the light in me come through to teach the world the truth about myself."

"I am one Self, in perfect harmony with all there is and all that there will be."

"I am one Self, and it is given me to feel this Self now within me and to cast all my illusions out of the one mind that is this Self."

Pause now to feel this one Self. Be vigilant and do not forget your goal.

Thank Jesus for teaching you truth, for His continued guidance, and for leading the way and transcending the ego.

Slowly come back and becoming aware of your surroundings. Turn your palms down and move your hands and feet. Open your eyes when you are ready.

Chapter 7

Answer the following questions about your perfect partner.

What do I like to do and would I enjoy doing with my partner?

_____
_____
_____
_____
_____

What vision or goals do my partner and I have in common?

_____
_____
_____
_____
_____

What religion would I like my partner to have?_____

What values and traits do you want your partner to have? Maybe it is also how do you define love because love is expressed through these values. If you recall, the Bible definition of love was referenced in chapter 3. Here are some attributes you may consider, and you can add your own that resonate with you.

_____Trust	_____Honesty/Truthfulness	_____Commitment
_____Hope	_____Wants to be together	_____Friendship
_____Support	_____Forgiving Nature	_____Loyalty
_____Patience	_____Kindness	_____Humbleness
_____Affection	_____Generosity	_____Concern for others' well-being
_____Protection	_____Acceptance	

_____ _____ _____ _____
_____ _____ _____ _____

Creative Visualization Meditation of Your Perfect Partner

Sitting tall in a comfortable position, take in a deep breath, completely filling your stomach, lungs, and chest. Pause and let it out completely exhaling pressing the belly button to the spine. Again, take a deep breath in and let it out, pulling the belly button to the spine.

Now close your eyes as you inhale and exhale. Breathe in and out, focusing on the breath and the tip of your nose. Follow the breath going in and out as you settle down, breathing in and out. Connect to the breath as you breathe rhythmically and become more relaxed. You are now relaxed.

Bring to mind a tranquil place that makes you feel relaxed. Maybe you envision a beach, a garden, a waterfall, or something similar. Feel your surroundings: the air, sand, water, or grass. Hear the noises: birds, waves, or water falling. See your surroundings. Are there flowers, trees, sand, and water?

Allow a beautiful golden light come down from heaven and enter your crown chakra and move down into your heart. Move your focus from the mind down to your heart center. Open your heart and allow this light energy to expand and surround you. Feel the warmth and support of this energy. Know you are safe and completely relaxed in the light.

Now, see yourself being with your dream partner.

What does he or she look like? Height, size, hair color, eye color, and so on?
What is he or she wearing?
What are you wearing?
Where are you going?
What are you doing?
What is the weather like?
Do you feel a breeze, the sun, or rain?
What sounds do you hear around you?
What smells do you smell?

What do you see around you?

How do you feel being with him or her?

What is it like to be with him or her?

How does he or she treat you?

How do you treat him or her?

What is he or she saying to you?

What are you saying to him or her?

If the following affirmations resonate with you, repeat them to yourself, or you can create your own that resonate with you.

I feel his or her unconditional love and support for me.

I see his or her generosity and patience toward me and others.

I see us communicating effectively and respecting each other's opinions.

I hear his or her encouraging words that support me in being my authentic self.

I feel his or her affection toward me and life.

I love how he or she is trustworthy, humble, honest, loyal, and kind.

I love how he or she makes me feel and how he or she lifts me up. Sit for a moment, allowing these feelings to sink into all your cells.

As your time is winding down, you hug and kiss your partner.

You leave him or her, and you feel wonderful. Just being with this person builds you up and encourages you to be the best person you can be.

As you leave, you think of one thing that you can do that honors yourself that you can start working on right now.

You feel better about yourself, encouraged, excited, and happy to finally be with your perfect partner.

Slowly come back and become aware of your surroundings. Turn your palms down and move your hands and feet. Open your eyes when you are ready.

P A R T N E R A S S E S S M E N T E X E R C I S E

What attracted you to this person?

_____

_____

What qualities did you not like about this person? It is OK if these are also what initially attracted you.

_____

_____

Which of the qualities that attracted you to this person are *not* listed in your answers to the exercise on attracting your perfect partner?

_____

_____

Did you list any of the qualities that you do not like in the exercise on attracting your perfect partner? Y____N____

Chapter 8

Meditation Prayer to the Holy Spirit

Sitting tall in a comfortable position, take in a deep breath, completely filling your stomach, chest, and lungs, pause, and exhale letting it out completely pressing belly button to spine. Again, take a deep breath in, pause, and exhale letting it out completely pressing belly button to spine.

Now close your eyes as you inhale and exhale. Breathe in and out, focusing on the breath and the tip of your nose. Follow the breath going in and out as you settle down, breathing in and out. Connect to the breath as you breathe rhythmically and become more relaxed. You are now relaxed.

Allow a beautiful gold light to come down from heaven and enter your crown chakra and move down into your heart. Move your focus from the mind to your heart center. Open your heart and allow this light energy to expand and surround you. Feel the warmth and support of this divine energy. Know you are safe, protected, and completely relaxed in the light.

Call upon Jesus now, who is your teacher and companion. Wait quietly with expectancy for Jesus's presence.

Jesus is speaking to you:
The Holy Spirit is the voice of God.
He shares God's will with you.
Your willingness to heal and to make yourself whole opens your ears to the voice of the Holy Spirit, whose message is wholeness.
Inviting the Holy Spirit in, welcoming Him, and providing protection shows Him that you want Him.
The Holy Spirit remembers what God's will is for you, so ask Him and He will tell you.
Trust the Holy Spirit because He speaks for you.

Just by offering Him a little place, He will lighten it so much that you will gladly let it be increased. You will begin to remember creation.

Turn toward the light, for the little spark in you is part of a light so great that it can sweep you out of darkness forever.

Let's pray to the Holy Spirit now:

O, Holy Spirit, beloved of my soul, I adore you.
Enlighten me, guide me, strengthen me, console me.
Tell me what I should do. Give me Your orders.
I promise to submit myself to all that You desire of me and to accept all that You permit to happen to me.
Let me only know Your will.[20]

Slowly come back and become aware of your surroundings. Turn your palms down and move your hands and feet. Open your eyes when you are ready.

You can e-mail me at soulbodynourishment@gmail.com for an audio version of the meditations, which includes background music to enhance your experience.

Conclusion

Our upbringing has taught us beliefs about who we think we are and how to be accomplished. These beliefs for most of us come from our ego-identified self and not from our authentic self. So we look outside ourselves for love, acceptance, worthiness, and happiness, leaving a void within. We are definitely here on a journey of trying to find what we are looking for. As long as you look outside of yourself, you will always feel depressed, unhappy, incomplete, inadequate, and like something is missing. As you turn inward now, pay attention to how you feel and own only the loving thoughts. The negative thoughts are ego and will talk you out of knowing your truth. If you can become more present, you will start to feel more happiness, love, joy, and peace. The more you seek it, the more it shows up. The ego becomes vicious as it fights for survival. Know you are on the right path. You can never go wrong when your decisions and words come from love.

Our journey to truth of who we are, why we are here, and what our purpose is in this physical reality here on earth is not an easy one. The most important point that I can stress to you is that you are *not* alone. You never have been, even though it feels like it through the separation in the mind. Every one of us is connected to each other and the universe. We all matter and are so important—more than you can ever realize or even imagine. We each have a place in the mind of God that can only be filled by each one of us. Because we are One in the Sonship, salvation needs every one of us. If just one of us is missing, we are not whole and not complete.

We are created from love and therefore are love. We create by extending love. This is why we feel good when we help each other, are nice to each other, and give to each other. As you share and give to one another, you receive what you have given. However, when your thoughts and actions come from ego, then you go against your truth, causing yourself to be out of alignment with who you are. This is why you do not feel good about your thoughts and actions.

If your brothers are part of you and you blame them for your deprivation, you are blaming yourself. And you cannot blame yourself without blaming them. That is why blame must be undone.[21] Self-blame comes from ego and you cannot enter God's Presence if you attack His Son.[22]

While you may not feel worthy, know that you are worthy because you are the Son or Daughter of God. Know that everyone of us is equal because we are one. Materialistic things do not measure your worthiness but *who* you are does.

While you may not feel loved, know that you are loved and are loved for infinity because you are made from love and extend love. The more you can express love to yourself and others, the better you will feel because you are honoring your authentic self. It is who you are. How can you deny yourself love? Look yourself in the mirror every day and say, "I love you."

While you may feel inadequate, know that you are enough just as you are because of who you are and whose you are. You were created in your Father's image, fully equipped with everything you need to fulfill your purpose.

Only you can deprive yourself of anything. Do not oppose this realization, for it is truly the beginning of the dawn of light. Remember also that the denial of this simple fact takes many forms, and these you must learn to recognize and to oppose steadfastly, without exception.[23]

This is why you have to live in the present moment, being aware at all times of what is happening as you are choosing your thoughts and actions. It truly is a process because we are always evolving and expanding. This is why you have to enjoy the journey and be kind and loving to yourself.

As you love yourself and accept yourself exactly the way you are, you will feel better about yourself. You will start to realize that your thoughts and beliefs are creating your reality. As you forgive and extend love to your brother, you will feel joy, happiness, and peace. Each of these actions are steps toward healing. The more you practice, the better learner and teacher you become. What you value is what you put your attention and resources toward. You are so worthy, and investing your time and resources into developing a relationship with yourself is the most important battle you will ever fight. Know that the ego does not give up easily. As you get closer to truth, you will see its fight for survival. Just be patient and loving to yourself when you feel you listened to the wrong voice. Know that there are no mistakes, and it takes practice to tune into your inner guidance system and to trust the guidance that you receive.

As you change your perception, your whole outer world will change. As you become your authentic self, you will become the best version of you!

This is why it really is ALL about YOU!

Share your light by Leaving a review on Amazon

How has your life changed since reading this book and doing the exercises and meditations? I am honored that you are recommending the book and leaving your feedback on Amazon! You are now making a difference by sharing your light to someone who is also walking in darkness. I am so grateful.

Namaste (The divine light in me honors the divine light in you).

PARTNERING TO BECOME THE BEST VERSION OF YOU

I know there is a lot of information in this book, and it feels overwhelming. Your ego will tell you lies and try to talk you out of change so it can remain in control. But remember how ego makes you feel when it is in control, and let this reminder push you forward on your path of love.

I love helping professional women who feel inadequate and are ready to be the best version of themselves. As a board-certified holistic health coach (AADP), I am here to partner with you and support you on this transformational journey through private sessions, speaking engagements, and seminars/workshops. I am here to serve and flexible to assist. Please do not hesitate to contact me with questions, inquiries, information on services, or how I can be of service.

E-mail: soulbodynourishment@gmail.com
Facebook page: www.facebook.com/SoulBodyNourishment
Website: www.soulbodynourishment.com

Nurturing yourself is unique and based on bio-individuality. My focus is healing from the inside out because everything we see externally is a true reflection of what is going on internally.

Remember, change will not happen overnight; it is a daily practice of mindfulness that brings about the change that you desire. If you pay attention, you will notice subtle changes and eventually big shifts as you acknowledge the changes occurring.

It is my honor to share my tips and tools with you in helping you become the best version of you.

This book is a result of my experience at the Institute for Integrative Nutrition (IIN), where I received my training in holistic wellness and health coaching. IIN offers a truly comprehensive health coach training program that invites students to deeply explore the things that are most nourishing to them. IIN explores the physical aspects of nutrition and eating wholesome foods that work best for each individual person as well as the concept of *primary food*—the idea that everything in life, including our spirituality, career, relationships, and fitness contributes to our inner and outer health. IIN introduced to me this concept of primary foods which I did not understand at the time how they affected my health. Since then, I have been on an inward journey, seeking to fill the void within and finding balance and optimal health, happiness, and love in the process. IIN changed my life, and I am forever grateful. I have always felt that I have a desire to help others, but I did not know how. This inner journey gave me clarity, strength, confidence, understanding, and passion that compels me to share what I've learned and to inspire others.

Beyond personal health, IIN offers training in health coaching as well as in business and marketing. Students who choose to pursue this field professionally complete the program and become equipped with the communication skills and branding knowledge they need to create a fulfilling career based on encouraging and supporting others in reaching their own health goals.

From renowned wellness experts as visiting teachers to the convenience of their online learning platform, this school has changed my life, and I believe it will do the same for you. I invite you to learn more about the Institute for Integrative Nutrition and explore how the health coach training program can help you transform your life by going to my website now:

www.soulbodynourishment.com and clicking on the tab **Become a Health Coach.**

HOPEFUL HEARTS MINISTRY
GIVING A VOICE TO SURVIVORS OF ABUSE

Founded by Shannon M. Deitz, survivor, international speaker, and author

www.HopefulHeartsMinistry.com

Hopeful Hearts Ministry was founded in 2011 by Shannon Deitz when she decided to step away from her parish ministry to have more time for speaking engagements and to start Hopeful Hearts. Her purpose in founding Hopeful Hearts is to help give a voice to those who can't speak out and to help and encourage survivors of abuse. Shannon also speaks at events such as retreats and seminars for women's groups across the United States.

Hopeful Hearts Ministry is an advocacy nonprofit organization [(501(c)(3)] that gives a voice to survivors of abuse. The ministry exists to help others understand their worth and realize their full potential while also providing programs that empower and serve to educate and improve the lives of those similarly victimized.

Hopeful Hearts Ministry aids in the long-term recovery of survivors of abuse through peer support sessions, programs, counseling, and public awareness events and videos. Their faith-based care alleviates suffering and helps restore confidence and self-worth.

The vision of Hopeful Hearts Ministry is for survivors of abuse to:

- Recognize the abuse suffered, bringing it into the light
- Receive compassionate support from a trusted peer
- Realize that the abuse they have endured does not define them
- Rise above victimization, embrace their full potential, and thrive

In proud support of Hopeful Hearts Ministry, I am donating a book to each survivor partnering with them because of your purchase.

Purchasing this book is directly helping survivors of abuse. It shows them they are not alone and that someone cares. It gives them hope and gives them tools to become empowered and overcome their past.

I express my heartfelt gratitude to you for being the hope and light to someone else who is walking in the darkness right now and does not see another way.

Notes

1. Marianne Williamson, *A Return to Love: Reflections on the Principles of a Course in Miracles (ACIM).* Excerpt from her book provided from Institute of Integrative Nutrition training material.

2. Don Miguel Ruiz, *The Mastery of Love: A Practical Guide to the Art of Relationship* (San Rafael, CA: Amber-Allen Publishing, 1999), loc 561, 578, and 594.

3. Don Miguel Ruiz, *The Mastery of Love: A Practical Guide to the Art of Relationship* (San Rafael, CA: Amber-Allen Publishing, 1999), loc 544.

4. Foundation for Inner Peace, Workbook for students section in *A Course in Miracles* (Mill Valley, CA: Foundation for Inner Peace, 2007), Lesson 66 7:2–4, 111.

5. Foundation for Inner Peace, Text section in *A Course in Miracles* (Mill Valley, CA: Foundation for Inner Peace, 2007), Chapter 3 VII 4:1, 50.

6. Foundation for Inner Peace, Text section in *A Course in Miracles* (Mill Valley, CA: Foundation for Inner Peace, 2007), Chapter 3 VII 5:1–4, 50.

7. https://www.biblegateway.com/passage/?search=1+Corinthians+13:4-8, The Holy Bible, New International Version (NIV), I Corinthians 13:4–8.

8. Shri Mataji Nirmala Devi, *Sahajayoga pamphlet*: Exploring the Inner System, The Seven Chakras.

9. https://www.cdc.gov/nchs/fastats/deaths.html, *National Vital Statistics Reports,* June 30, 2016.

10. Dr. Mark Hyman, Expert in Functional Medicine, Institute of Integrative Nutrition training material.

11. http://www.creationsmagazine.com/articles/C113/Hicks.html, Jerry and Esther Hicks, "The Universal Law of Attraction: Defined," *Creations Magazine.*

12. http://blog.mindvalleyacademy.com/happiness-and-positive-living/charlie-chaplins-love-manifesto; MindValley Academy Blog, *Charlie Chaplin's Love Yourself Manifesto (Infographic).*

13. Catherine Marshall, *The Prayer of Relinquishment* (Guideposts, January 2015), 48–51.

14. Foundation for Inner Peace, Introduction in *A Course in Miracles* (Mill Valley, CA: Foundation for Inner Peace, 2007).

15. Foundation for Inner Peace, Text section in *A Course in Miracles* (Mill Valley, CA: Foundation for Inner Peace, 2007), Chapter 8 VIII 8:6–8, 157.

16. Foundation for Inner Peace, Text section in *A Course in Miracles* (Mill Valley, CA: Foundation for Inner Peace, 2007), Chapter 8 VI 9:6–10, 150.

17. https://www.biblegateway.com/passage/?search=Exodus+20&version=KJV, The Holy Bible, King James Version (KJV), Exodus 20:3.

18. https://www.biblegateway.com/passage/?search=Matthew+6%3A19-21&version=NIV, The Holy Bible, New International Version (NIV), Matthew 6:19–21.

19. https://www.biblegateway.com/passage/?search=Matthew+22%3A37-39&version=KJV, The Holy Bible, King James Version (KJV), Matthew 22:37, 39.

20. http://www.czestochowa.us/component/page,shop.product_details/flypage, flypage-ask.tpl/product_id,281/category_id,181/option, com_virtuemart/Itemid,55/; *The Holy Spirit Prayer Card.*

21. Foundation for Inner Peace, Text section in *A Course in Miracles* (Mill Valley, CA: Foundation for Inner Peace, 2007), Chapter 11 God or the Ego IV 5:1–3, 201.

22. Foundation for Inner Peace, Text section in *A Course in Miracles* (Mill Valley, CA: Foundation for Inner Peace, 2007), Chapter 11 God or the Ego IV 5:6, 201.

23. Foundation for Inner Peace, Text section in *A Course in Miracles* (Mill Valley, CA: Foundation for Inner Peace, 2007), Chapter 11 God or the Ego IV 4:1–3, 201.

About the Author

Debra Stoltz is a board-certified holistic health coach with the American Association of Drugless Practitioners (AADP) and owner of SoulBody Nourishment. She has received a health coaching certification from the Institue of Integrative Nutrition and a Basic Mat Pilates certification from Peak Pilates. She has a Bachelor of Arts in accounting from the University of West Florida (UWF), a Texas-licensed Certified Public Accountant, and a member of Texas Society of Certified Public Accountants (TSCPA). She is also a lightworker and facilitates A Course In Miracles (ACIM) in the Humble/Kingwood, Texas, area.

As a single mom, raising two kids and maintaining an accounting career for more than twenty years, she ran herself in the ground, feeling completely exhausted. She was desperate for help in 2008 and started seeking out information about health and wellness. She is so grateful to be on this journey and for this opportunity to serve her family, friends, community, and humanity as a health and wellness resource.

She knows what it is like to have health issues, relationship issues, feel inadequate, and looking for love and happiness outside yourself trying to fill the void you feel within. She believes in a daily meditation practice, physical activity, a gluten-free, dairy-free, organic, whole grain diet, and is working on her next book, *Nourishing Your Soul's Temple.*

She is passionate to share her personal journey of searching for love, health, and happiness and be the light to others. It is her mission to share her tools and tips of how to be the best version of yourself.

For more information on Debbie and her services,
visit her website: www.soulbodynourishment.com or
e-mail her at: soulbodynourishment@gmail.com

www.ingramcontent.com/pod-product-compliance
Lightning Source LLC
LaVergne TN
LVHW021539080426
835509LV00019B/2727